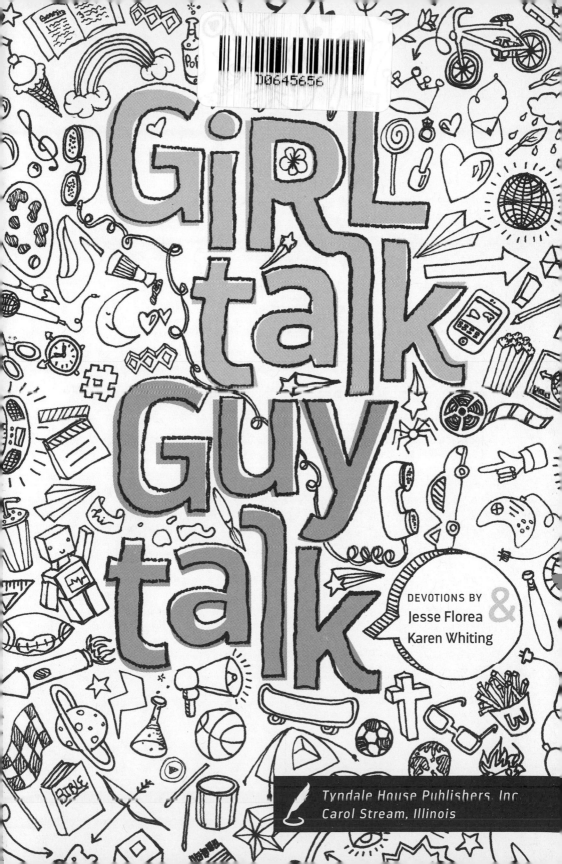

GiRL talk #Guy talk

DEVOTIONS BY Jesse Florea & Karen Whiting

Tyndale House Publishers, Inc.
Carol Stream, Illinois

Visit Tyndale online at www.tyndale.com.

Visit Karen Whiting online at www.karenwhiting.com.

Visit Jesse Florea online at christianauthorsnetwork.com/jesse-florea.

TYNDALE and Tyndale's quill logo are registered trademarks of Tyndale House Publishers, Inc.

Girl Talk Guy Talk: Devotions for Teens

Copyright © 2017 by Karen Whiting and Jesse Florea. All rights reserved.

Cover and interior illustrations by Emma VanWagner. Copyright © Tyndale House Publishers, Inc. All rights reserved.

Designed by Julie Chen

For information about special discounts for bulk purchases, please contact Tyndale House Publishers at csresponse@tyndale.com, or call 1-800-323-9400.

ISBN 978-1-4964-1786-2

Printed in the United States of America

23	22	21	20	19	18	17
7	6	5	4	3	2	1

To my almost-teen grandsons, Joseph Pena and Ethan

Whiting. I pray you'll develop great communication

skills and continue following the Lord.

—K. W.

For Ari and Katie, my two favorite nieces.

Enjoy all the adventures and excitement of your teen years.

Always remember you are loved by your family and by God.

—J. F.

Contents

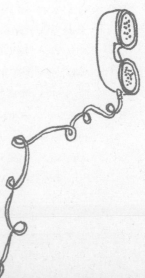

PART ONE

The True You

Growing up isn't just about more birthdays or reaching the age to drive or vote.

That part is easy. Getting older happens naturally. Becoming the true you, on the other hand, takes effort. God knows the true you. He wants to see *that* you grow. He wants your relationships to thrive so you can be happy and spread his love.

Being real is the first part of building healthy relationships. The next part is connecting to others through communicating. That includes expressing who you are and what you believe, as well as valuing the words and thoughts of others.

As you jump into this book, be ready to think about who you are and the person you want to become. You may need to answer some important questions:

- What do I value?
- How can I best use my words to connect with people?
- What do I want in life, and how can my words express that?

Answer honestly. Dig into what you truly believe. The goal of communication is understanding. This book will help you become a better communicator. It'll help you understand guys and girls; it will also help you understand yourself. Your true self, that is.

for Guys & Girls

CQ: Communication Quotient Quiz

Circle the answer that best describes you.

1. When I talk with someone of the opposite sex
   a. I can't open my mouth out of fear.
   b. I usually say something lame.
   c. It's easy for me, since I have brothers/sisters.
   d. I feel comfortable because I enjoy a good chat.

2. The easiest topic to talk about with someone of the opposite sex is
   a. school.
   b. sports.
   c. no topic. I can't talk to guys/girls.
   d. friends, hobbies, food, anything really.

3. If someone of the opposite sex is acting weird, I
   a. laugh.
   b. join in.
   c. get away fast.
   d. make fun of him/her.

4. When it comes to talking,
   a. I can easily monopolize the conversation.
   b. I speak only when asked a question.
   c. I talk half the time and listen the other half.
   d. I like to talk, but no one seems to listen.

5. When someone of the opposite sex talks to me, I
   a. look him/her in the eye and listen.
   b. look down at the floor.
   c. turn beet red and can hardly breathe.
   d. give the best response I can come up with quickly.

6. If I mess up and say something wrong in front of someone of the opposite sex,
   a. I giggle or say, "Oops, my bad!" and correct myself.
   b. I pretend it never happened.
   c. I clam up and stop talking.
   d. I smile, apologize, and start over.

7. If I like someone of the opposite sex,
   a. I smile and compliment him/her.
   b. I ask a friend to talk to him/her for me.
   c. I just daydream about him/her. I'm too afraid to talk to my crush.
   d. I ask questions to find out more about him/her.

8. If someone of the opposite sex hurts my feelings, I would
   a. avoid him/her.
   b. get angry.
   c. ask a friend to tell him/her how I feel.
   d. tell him/her that I'm hurt, since he/she probably doesn't have a clue.

9. I like a guy/girl who
   a. makes me laugh.
   b. is kind.
   c. is patient.
   d. actually likes me for me.

10. When someone of the opposite sex asks me a question, I
    a. mumble an answer.
    b. start to answer, then ramble on and on.
    c. answer and ask a question back.
    d. answer and wait for him/her to ask another question.

11. If the guy/girl I'm going out with wants to get physical, I
    a. escape and keep from being alone with that person.
    b. go with the flow.
    c. pull out my cell phone and show him/her some cat videos.
    d. explain why I choose to remain pure.

12. Breaking up is hard. It's best to
    a. be honest and say he/she has good qualities but explain that
       we're not the best match.
    b. avoid him/her until he/she gets the message.
    c. ask a friend to tell him/her.
    d. text him/her myself.

Answers:

1. a=1, b=2, c=3, d=4; 2. a=2, b=3, c=1, d=4; 3. a=3, b=4, c=2, d=1; 4. a=3, b=1, c=4, d=2; 5. a=4, b=2, c=1, d=3; 6. a=3, b=2, c=1, d=4; 7. a=3, b=2, c=1, d=4; 8. a=2, b=1, c=3, d=4; 9. a=4, b=4, c=4, d=4; 10. a=1, b=2, c=4, d=3; 11. a=3, b=1, c=2, d=4; 12. a=4, b=1, c=3, d=2.

Add up your score:

15–20 points. Looks like you have a real fear of talking with guys/girls and being around them. Try talking with people of the opposite sex in your youth group or another setting where you feel comfortable. You could even ask for some tips from your mom or dad. Relax a bit. The guys/girls you're talking to are probably afraid too.

21–30 points. You probably feel a bit awkward around guys/girls. You may even try to get friends to talk to them for you when you need to speak up (hint: this is rarely a good idea). Keep reading! You'll get lots more tips in this book.

31–40 points. You're fairly comfortable with guys/girls. Your reactions may still be a bit immature sometimes, but keep working at it.

41–48 points. You have a great maturity and comfort around guys/girls. You're confident and considerate. You're the one who helps guys and girls get more comfortable with one another. Maybe you could be a small group leader at church.

The right word spoken at the right time can be golden. People sometimes say that silence is golden, but a good conversation can be even more so. Communication is about choosing words that build relationships and connect with other people.

How'd you do on the quiz? (Tough way to start a book, right?) The good news is that plenty of the book is left, and communication is a skill you'll develop with practice.

WORD OF TRUTH

Like apples of gold in settings of silver is a word spoken in right circumstances.
PROVERBS 25:11, NASB

Girl talk **Laughing Matters**

What makes you laugh?

Videos of cats running into paper bags are pretty cute . . . and funny. A TV sitcom or romantic comedy can be good for a chuckle. Sometimes a well-told joke can tickle our funny bones.

Girl: So what do you want for Christmas?
Guy: A speaker system with a car wrapped around it.

Girl 1: Don't you wish you had a special guy in your life?
Girl 2: No, I'm willing to wait for my knight in shining armor.
Girl 1: I'd settle for one in aluminum foil.

Okay, those jokes may not make you laugh, but looking for the humorous side of life can make things more fun. Sometimes we can take friendship troubles, bad-hair days, and social-media likes too seriously. Sure, there's a time to buckle down and be serious. But don't be afraid to loosen up and enjoy the roller coasters of life.

Laughter is good medicine. Humor helps people cope and relieves tension. It's one of the best tools to keep relationships healthy, so it's good to develop a sense of humor if your hopes for the future include building a strong marriage. Guys tend to be better at laughing things off than girls—and it's been that way for a long time. In the Bible, Job was having one of the most terrible times ever. His friend Bildad said that God would fill his mouth with laughter. He trusted that Job would find humor in life again.

More recently a mom in Florida told her extended family that she and her son had survived a terrible hurricane by relying on God's Word, prayer, and a little laughter. During the storm, she'd read the Bible and prayed. After a while she came to the story of Jesus calming a storm. Suddenly, all the noise outside stopped. Following a few minutes of silence, the boy said, "You should have read that one first, Mom."

When you're in a stressful situation, look around to find something silly. Look for something to laugh about. By developing your sense of humor, you'll be able to see the funny side of life. And people may have an easier time getting to know you.

WORD OF TRUTH

He will once again fill your mouth with laughter and your lips with shouts of joy.

JOB 8:21

Got a Funny Feeling?

Who do you think a girl would rather go out with?

a. Bozo the Clown
b. Albert Einstein

They've both got great hair. But the answer is *a*. Girls like funny guys more than smart guys. That's what a national men's magazine found when they surveyed more than one thousand women. This same study also discovered that kindness ranked high as a character trait.

The problem with a lot of humor is that it's not kind. It's cutting and cruel. It puts down and pokes fun. Mimicking the way somebody talks may make your friends laugh on the outside, but most people don't really appreciate that kind of humor.

The Bible doesn't either. Ephesians 5:4 says, "Obscene stories, foolish talk, and coarse jokes—these are not for you."

Many popular comedians cross the line into cussing or telling inappropriate stories to get a laugh. It's natural to want to repeat their jokes to your friends, but you don't have to follow in their footsteps. Look for things that are truly funny, like when a cat runs into a paper bag. (Just kidding.)

A lot of humor comes down to individual preference. Some people love slapstick. Others enjoy a good pun. Your taste in humor can change as you grow.

You probably thought this joke was hilarious when you were a kid:

Q: Why should students wear glasses when they do math?
A: To improve di-vision.

(Okay, that's still hilarious. But you've probably outgrown chickens crossing the road.)

So as you hang out with girls, try to discover what kind of humor they like. Maybe you can joke about your favorite movie or TV show. Or they may enjoy hearing an embarrassing story about you. Keep in mind that kindness and humor should go hand in hand. Your friends want to laugh with you—not at somebody's expense.

So if a girl laughs at your gross joke, know she's probably not laughing on the inside. Instead she may be thinking, *This isn't the kind of guy that I want to be with.*

WORD OF TRUTH

Obscene stories, foolish talk, and coarse jokes—these are not for you. Instead, let there be thankfulness to God.
EPHESIANS 5:4

Girl Talk

What's Your Rep?

Have you ever stood near someone who reeked? You probably got away as fast as possible. A bad reputation, like a bad smell, can also cause people to avoid us.

What people think of us can make a difference, for good or bad. Some girls are known for their brains, kindness, style, or athletic ability. Others might be known for being a flirt or for how far they'll go with guys.

Sometimes a reputation is based on facts. Other times rumors and lies paint the wrong picture of a person. Do you know what people say about you? Ask a few friends what they know about your reputation. List words used to describe you:

_____

Now think of words you want to be associated with your name: _____

Do the lists match up? If not, try these tactics:

• Gossip and rumors usually die down if you don't feed them. Ignore the lies and work on developing your character.
• If lies spread, know you're not alone. Nearly one out of five high school girls have been victims of sexual rumors.
• Rebuilding your reputation takes time. Work on it, one person at a time. Make sure your true friends have the real story and enlist their help with combating the rumors.
• If things get really intense, ask a parent or other trusted adult for help. You don't have to deal with this alone.

Overcome the past . . .

- If there's truth behind your bad reputation, be honest—admit you've made mistakes, and tell people you've chosen to change.
- Almost half of Facebook timeline pages have profanity. Delete the junk that others post on your space. You can also ask good friends to post positive comments about you to drown out negative voices.
- If necessary, seek out new friends who will not judge you based on the past.
- Get advice from someone who is older and wiser than you are. Ask a mature Christian to walk with you on your journey to a new reputation.

Build a good rep . . .

- Be genuine and caring toward others.
- Focus on developing godly character traits:
  - Dress modestly.
  - Use clean language.
  - Don't tease.
  - Keep your word.
  - Avoid solo dates or being alone with a guy.

Like a sweet perfume that leaves a pleasant scent, let your character leave a good impression on the people around you.

WORD OF TRUTH

A good reputation is more valuable than costly perfume.
ECCLESIASTES 7:1

Guy talk

Protect Your Rep

What do you want to be known for? Do you want to be the guy who can throw down a monster dunk? (If so, you better start working on your vertical leap.) Or maybe you want to be the class clown. Some guys want to go out with as many girls as they can. Others just want to be the cool guy who never lets anything bother him.

Take some time to think, and then write down what you want to be known for: _____

_____

_____

_____

_____

As a Christ follower, your reputation is important. You might be the only Christian some people know. Their opinion of you will influence their view of Jesus. That's why King Solomon wrote, "A good reputation is more valuable than costly perfume" (Ecclesiastes 7:1).

If you're having trouble coming up with traits that you want to be known for, think about these qualities of Christ:

- Conviction. Know what God's Word says about what's right and wrong, and live according to those beliefs. Jesus stood for his convictions to the point of willingly dying on the cross. There was no compromise in Christ.

- Responsibility. Do you make excuses, or do you follow through on your commitments? Take responsibility for your actions, admit when you're wrong, and always be trustworthy.
- Understanding. Jesus knew God. (After all, he *was* God.) Understanding God and his grace is one of the most important things we can do to build our character.
- Cooperation. How do you help your friends? Who supports you? Jesus surrounded himself with trusted friends who could help when times got tough. And he made his friends better by encouraging them to grow closer to God.

If you haven't already, make a plan to build and then protect your reputation. When you take the step to pep up your rep, you'll have more success in life . . . and with the ladies.

WORD OF TRUTH

A good reputation is more valuable than costly perfume.
ECCLESIASTES 7:1

Pop Quiz!

Take this true-or-false quiz:

True / False   1. Guys flock around me.

True / False   2. I have plenty of friends, so I'm not worried about popularity.

True / False   3. I have a close friend, but sometimes I wish I had more friends.

True / False   4. I feel lonely and maybe even cast out by popular kids.

What you marked to the above questions doesn't really matter. There are no right or wrong answers. What matters is that it's great to hang out with friends. They make us laugh. They share with us. They listen to us and care about what we say.

It really hurts to feel overlooked, like you blend into the scenery. But life at the top of the popularity food chain isn't all that it seems either. Popularity comes with pitfalls. It can be fleeting and fickle. So no matter how you answered the questions, don't ever give up on making new friends.

Think about this . . .

- If you have a few friends, you are rich! Be thankful for the ones you have, and remember why you like them. Be open to others, but don't make becoming part of the "in crowd" a goal.

- Jesus spent forty days in a desert, alone. After that, he surrounded himself with friends for the rest of his ministry. He understood loneliness. He found his worth in God. And he knew what it took to find good friends. Follow his footsteps.
- The best way to make friends is to be a friend. Smile, be kind, and be open to talking to people. Seek friends who share your interests by joining groups related to your passions and hopes for the future.
- Be confident. Lift up your head and remember that God will always love you. When the time is right, he'll send the right people into your life.
- If you're already super popular, be gracious and kind. Be a good example of how to treat people. Don't put others down just to stay on top. Widen your circle of friends. Then you'll be an even better friend.

WORD OF TRUTH

Oh, dear Corinthian friends! We have spoken honestly with you, and our hearts are open to you.
2 CORINTHIANS 6:11

Popular Opinion

There's no secret recipe for popularity. If there was a chemical formula, the science geniuses would figure it out, mix up a batch, and spray it all over their bodies. (Note: those Axe body spray commercials *aren't* real.)

When you look around, you probably notice the most intelligent students don't have the largest followings. If an equation were written, it might look like this:

$$\text{Wisdom} > \text{Popularity}$$

Jocks often find themselves at the top of the popularity food chain (not that jocks are necessarily dumb). Those deemed extremely attractive also make it into the inner circle. Life can look easier for this elite group—good things just seem to happen to them.

Have you ever wondered why so many girls go for the popular guys? You could ask a girl. But just asking the question could cast you into the pit of unpopularity, and climbing out can be slippery. Once you're in the "out group," it's hard to get back out (or would that be "in"?).

While there's no chemical concoction to make yourself popular, there actually may be a formula. If you turn yourself into a scientist and study the popular group, you can come to some conclusions.

Most popular people are outgoing. Having a lot of friends is hard if you're shy. The "cool" kids stand out in a crowd instead of shrinking back. These students are confident. They're at ease with themselves. They have an air of power. Being around them can be exciting.

In the same way popularity can be recognized, your faith in Christ should get you noticed. The list of traits just looks a little bit different. The apostle Paul records qualities that help you stand out. Read that list in Galatians 5:22-23. Where do you need to grow? Would you like to be more at peace with yourself? Do you need to show more kindness? Write down three characteristics to work on: _____,
_____, _____.

When it comes to showing these traits, the equation looks like this:

$$\text{Fruit of the Spirit} = \text{Reflecting God}$$

And that's a formula worth following.

WORD OF TRUTH

The Holy Spirit produces this kind of fruit in our lives: love, joy, peace, patience, kindness, goodness, faithfulness, gentleness, and self-control.
GALATIANS 5:22-23

Girl talk

Life without Regrets

Wouldn't it be great to always say and do the right thing? As humans we stumble, put our big toe in our mouths, and sometimes make bad choices. Think about times you wish you had a giant eraser that would wipe out hurtful words or mistakes. Imagine how much easier life would become:

- You gossiped about a friend or shared something told to you in confidence. Then the person found out what you said and confronted you. Just take out your eraser. Whew! A clean slate.
- You took a dare and sent a mean text to a new girl. Erase. The deed is forever undone.

What a relief that would be. But that's not reality . . . and that's actually a good thing.

God doesn't want us to forget our mistakes. He wants us to learn from them and become more like him. Instead of giving us erasers, he offers us forgiveness. We can confess our sins to him and be forgiven. Then we can confess to the people we hurt and ask them for forgiveness. The person may not be able to forgive you right away. When you hurt someone, he or she loses trust in you. But taking responsibility for your words and actions shows a level of maturity on your part and a desire to make things right. You can feel at peace about that.

Remember that your past mistakes provide valuable lessons. You'll become more compassionate and responsible if you learn from poor choices or missteps you've made in the past. Then the forgiveness God offers you frees you of guilt and lets you move forward and make better choices. It's a fresh start . . . without regrets.

WORD OF TRUTH

I confessed all my sins to you and stopped trying to hide my guilt. I said to myself, "I will confess my rebellion to the LORD." And you forgave me! All my guilt is gone.

PSALM 32:5

No Regrets

Have you ever done something you wished you could take back? Every guy has. Life doesn't have a rewind button . . . but what if it did?

- You're doing research for a homework assignment and accidentally click one of those ads on the side of the screen. A website pops up that you *definitely* shouldn't be looking at. You linger a bit too long before clicking out of it. Now you've got an image stuck in your head. Hit the back arrow. Instant rewind. Image gone. Website never seen.
- A group of guys is talking about a girl in your class. The conversation gets a bit R-rated. You make a comment that makes everybody laugh. Inside, you cringe at yourself. Click the back arrow. Instant rewind. You walk past the group of guys without joining the conversation.

That'd be kind of cool. But God has given you something better than a rewind button. It's called forgiveness. Instead of trying to undo your mistakes, you can bring good out of them by seeking forgiveness and changing your actions in the future.

The apostle Paul made plenty of mistakes, including killing Christians and doubting that Jesus is God's Son. He could've become trapped by his guilt. But he discovered there are two kinds of grief—one good and one bad. "Godly grief produces a repentance that leads to salvation without regret,"

Paul wrote in 2 Corinthians 7:10 (ESV), "whereas worldly grief produces death."

The guilt we feel after messing up may actually be a good thing. God wants us to experience the consequences of our actions so that we will change in the future. The purpose of godly grief is to help us turn away from bad decisions and move forward in a positive way.

But what about the guilt that makes you feel helpless and worthless? That's definitely not from God. Those feelings can make you think, *There's no way God could love me after what I did.*

That's a lie. The truth is that God wants you to live without regret. He wants you to know and experience his life-changing grace. Don't dwell on past failures. Look forward to godly successes.

In God's wisdom, he didn't put a rewind button in our lives . . . just a way forward.

WORD OF TRUTH

Godly grief produces a repentance that leads to salvation without regret, whereas worldly grief produces death.
2 CORINTHIANS 7:10, ESV

Girl Talk

Be You!

People don't like pretenders. Instead of trying to be a person you think someone else might like, it's best to be yourself from the start. Don't change who you are to try to please a guy. That never works. (Okay, it might work for a while, but you'll eventually be found out.) Be you and be real!

But, you may wonder, *who am I really?* During these years, you are still discovering and becoming the real you . . . the person God created you to be.

As you grow into your true self, keep in mind these keys to being a loving person:

Be honest, but kind.
Be helpful, not selfish.
Be considerate, not mean.
Be loyal, not a gossip.
Be forgiving, not angry or hurtful.

To be you, accept who you are and how God made you. It's okay if you are naturally (circle the words that describe you) . . .

talkative / a quiet listener
funny / serious
tall / medium / short
shy / outgoing
spontaneous / careful and intentional

someone who comes alive in group settings / someone who prefers one-on-one talks

a bookworm / a sports nut

Add more words that describe you:

_____   _____

_____   _____

Believe in yourself and the dreams God gives you. Be curious to get to know yourself deep down. Develop your good qualities, always seeking to be more like Christ.

Remember, God knows the real you, and he loves and accepts you!

WORD OF TRUTH

Thank you for making me so wonderfully complex! Your workmanship is marvelous—how well I know it.
PSALM 139:14

Guy talk
The Value of You

"Life's hard. It's even harder when you're stupid."

Actor John Wayne reportedly said these words in an interview when asked what advice he'd give to students. For decades, John Wayne was one of the biggest actors in Hollywood. His characters were tough, honest, and real. Years after he died, a book about him was published called *John Wayne: The Genuine Article*.

That's what he was—genuine. He said what he meant and meant what he said. That's a good way to live.

As guys, we should act the same way—genuinely. But too often, we find ourselves following the crowd to be cool. We stray away from our true selves as we try to fit in.

Have you ever (check all that apply) . . .

- ☐ laughed at a crude joke, not because it was funny but because everybody else was laughing?
- ☐ worn a certain brand of clothing just because it was cool?
- ☐ acted one way around a girl and a different way around your friends?
- ☐ made fun of somebody because all your friends were doing it?

God didn't put you on this planet to be a clone of your peers. You're here to be *you*. The true you. If you don't know who that is, dig into the Bible, talk to a trusted friend, or sit down with your parents or youth pastor.

Girls want a guy who stands out . . . who's real.

God says the person he uniquely created you to be is extremely valuable to him.

Act that way. Act like *you* and be genuine.

 ## WORD OF TRUTH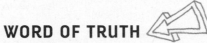

You are more valuable to God than a whole flock of sparrows.

MATTHEW 10:31

Girl talk: Words Begin in the Heart

Words are not simply sounds composed of stringing twenty-six letters together in different patterns.

Technically, what we hear comes from vibrations. The motion of the cords in our larynx, or voice box, creates sound that we learn to control and form into words. A baby babbles until she learns to imitate the people around her to speak a language.

But words aren't only sound. There's also emotion. Thought (or sometimes thoughtlessness) is involved too. So ultimately, words are thoughts expressed aloud—thoughts that begin in the heart. That's what Jesus was talking about in Matthew 12:34.

Think about what you've recently said to the guys (and girls) around you:

- Grumpy words—complaining or downcast thoughts that reflect depression and other negative feelings
- Encouraging words—the uplifting reflections of a person who feels happy and loved
- Angry words—yelling and dumping insulting or accusing words on the people around you

If you've been using a lot of angry or grumpy words, pause and try to discover where all the negativity is coming from. These words show there's something happening in your heart. Maybe you're hanging around with people who pull you down. Perhaps you're dragged down because your mom yelled at you, or you feel anger because someone hurt your BFF, or you are still dwelling on a hurt from last week. Let go and forgive people.

You can't change other people, but you can work on your heart, so that what flows out of it is beautiful. Begin with these HEART-healthy actions.

Hold on to healthy, happy thoughts.
Erase negative words with forgiveness.
Assure yourself that you are loved and accepted by God.
Reveal the real you.
Trust God in good times and bad (he is in control), and trust your loved ones.

Having a healthy heart begins with your relationship with God. God can handle your negative talk. Pour out your heart to him. Find strength and joy in his love. If you can't escape your negative talk and thoughts, have a conversation with your parents or youth pastor. They may have some ideas to help you.

WORD OF TRUTH

Whatever is in your heart determines what you say.
MATTHEW 12:34

Guy talk

Hey, That's Greeeat

Some guys wield their sarcastic tongues like a Jedi wields a lightsaber. They're always ready with a sarcastic remark, like these:

Mom: Why are your clothes still all over your floor?
You: Uh, gravity.

Girl: Hey, did you get a haircut?
You: Nope. I just dyed the tips to make them invisible.

Do you see any problem with these remarks? Sarcasm's funny, right?

Not to everybody. No matter how funny it might seem, a sarcastic comment can hurt the person it's aimed at. Imagine how it would feel to be on the receiving end of the two comments listed above. What do you think the next comment from Mom might be?

a. "Ha, ha. You're the funniest son ever."
b. "Very funny, Sir Isaac Newton. But if your stuff doesn't get picked up in the next five minutes, you're grounded."

It's probably going to be closer to *b*.

And how about the girl who tried to compliment your haircut? What would she say?

a. "I dye my hair too. We should go on a date."

b. "I'm sorry I noticed . . . jerk."

Again, the answer will probably be *b*. While girls like funny guys, they aren't necessarily attracted to sarcastic guys—including the sarcastic girls. Sarcastic remarks can hurt. Even if your friends or girls laugh at your sarcasm, they can be wounded on the inside, and that affects the way they see you.

One of the smartest guys in the Bible, King Solomon, wrote, "Some people make cutting remarks, but the words of the wise bring healing."

Would you rather bring a. hurt or b. healing with your words?

Go with choice *b*.

WORD OF TRUTH

Some people make cutting remarks, but the words of the wise bring healing.

PROVERBS 12:18

Girl talk

I Can't Decide

Some decisions are easy: *Do I want brownies or chocolate chip cookies?*

Obvious answer: Both!

But other decisions take more thought:

- *What do I want to do with my life?*
- *What college or career should I pursue?*
- *What do I say if a guy asks me to _____?*

There's no need to rush major choices that impact your future. We also shouldn't give in to pressure from someone who wants us to make a quick decision, especially if it involves dating.

Think about some decisions you're facing right now. Big or little, write them down: _____

_____

_____

_____

You might want to sit with a friend as you make tough choices about your future. Guys tend to be decisive and good listeners as you struggle with choices. Plus, most of them love to give their opinion.

Also, include your parents in your decision-making. They love you and care about your future as much as you do—maybe even more.

And as you think about big decisions, try these tips:

- Set a time when you'll be calm and can think clearly.
- List the choices, including pros and cons for each.
- Look in the Bible for similar situations.
- List the costs (time needed, money, supplies, impact on family and others).
- List the benefits (what you will gain and how it could help others).
- Pray about the choice.
- Ask yourself if you need more information and how to get it.
- Get input from parents, family friends, or wise friends.
- Decide on a time frame for a final decision.

By using your head, your heart, and your faith in making a decision, you'll be more confident in your choices. You'll also be able to communicate to others about why you made the decision you did.

And don't forget: once you decide, you've got to follow through. But first celebrate your great decision with some brownies . . . er, make that cookies.

WORD OF TRUTH

Don't begin until you count the cost. For who would begin construction of a building without first calculating the cost to see if there is enough money to finish it?
LUKE 14:28

Gray Matters

There's an obesity crisis, and you're at great risk!

But it's not what you think. Scientists in Japan performed magnetic resonance imaging scans (MRIs) on the brains of 276 kids who liked watching TV. The MRIs showed that the children who watched around four hours of TV per day had excess gray matter around their prefrontal cortex.

So what? you might think. *More gray matter is good.*

A big brain may be a beautiful thing, but scientists say building gray matter in this particular area is linked with lower verbal intelligence. Instead of bulky prefrontal cortexes, thin ones are better. Researchers say playing an instrument, creating art, writing stories, and doing other creative activities help the thinning process.

Hmmm, maybe that proves what our parents have been saying all along: watching TV does turn our brains to mush.

Studies show that many teens spend about nine hours a day staring at a screen. Whether it's a TV screen, cell phone screen, computer screen, or tablet screen, we're feeding our brains all the time. Many of these screen activities don't fully engage your brain.

Building a healthy brain doesn't happen by accident. We have to be thoughtful about what we think about. The Bible tells us to fix our minds on what is true, honorable, right, pure, lovely, admirable, excellent, and praiseworthy. When we dig into God's Word, have a deep conversation with a friend, play a board game, or walk through nature, it builds our minds in a good way.

Think about that list again:

- ☐ true
- ☐ honorable
- ☐ right
- ☐ pure
- ☐ lovely
- ☐ admirable
- ☐ excellent
- ☐ praiseworthy

Before you put something into your brain, make sure you can check some boxes on that list. As followers of Christ, we should be renewing our minds—not fattening them up. That may mean spending less time on various activities (TV watching, video games, social media) and using that time to build relationships with God and the people we care about.

WORD OF TRUTH

Fix your thoughts on what is true, and honorable, and right, and pure, and lovely, and admirable. Think about things that are excellent and worthy of praise.
PHILIPPIANS 4:8

Girl Talk Vote of Confidence

We don't always feel confident. A bad hair day can throw us off our game. A low grade after studying hard can make us feel like a failure. Annoying blemishes, clothes that don't fit right, or just the occasional blahs can rock our confidence and leave us feeling insecure.

But true confidence isn't associated with a feeling. Confidence comes from the fact that we are created by God with unique talents, looks, and thoughts. We may hear a lot about self-esteem. But God-esteem is way more consistent, helpful, and powerful. When we truly believe God loves us *and* loves how he created us, then we can be comfortable with who—and whose—we are.

And getting comfortable with who we are and how we're made is a big step toward becoming confident. Confidence shows in every area of our lives. Try these confidence-building tips:

- When you're talking to someone, keep your head up, look into his or her eyes, and smile. Your body language will display confidence.
- Dress in clothes that you think look good on you (and that you feel good in), but don't show too much. Being modest shows you are confident enough in your personality and thoughts that you don't need to rely on your physical attributes.
- Give yourself a pep talk to remind yourself you are valuable and have great qualities. Pray before tough conversations, asking God for confidence.

- If you have a differing idea on something that's being talked about, speak up and share it. Good guys appreciate girls who think for themselves.
- Surround yourself with friends who believe in you and support you.
- Really listen when someone speaks to you—don't daydream or think about what you're going to say next. Respond and ask questions.
- Look for guys who smile and show acceptance. If a guy really gets into a conversation with you, it can help build your confidence.

Even if you don't feel confident, act confident. God has already given you a vote of confidence, and you should do the same for yourself.

WORD OF TRUTH

Do not, therefore, fling away your fearless confidence, for it carries a great and glorious compensation of reward.
HEBREWS 10:35, AMPC

Choose to Ooze

Oozing doesn't sound attractive. An infected wound oozes. A popped pimple oozes. Slime oozes from spoiled meat. *Gross!*

But when you choose to ooze confidence, girls will be drawn to you. Girls like confident guys—guys who stand up for what they believe and speak their minds. Confident guys aren't afraid to stand out or look silly, so they take chances. They also aren't afraid to ask for help, because they know admitting that they don't know everything is a sign of strength, not weakness.

The Bible says we can be confident because God is always there to help us. Maybe people will make fun of us or mock our beliefs. But, really, does that hurt anything? No way. When our confidence comes from Christ, we're unstoppable.

Confidence starts with how we think. Even if we don't feel confident (and nobody does all the time), we can choose to be confident. A confident guy isn't afraid to talk with an outcast or fess up when he makes a mistake. He doesn't cringe when asked a question in class. He's ready and willing to take the last shot in a basketball game. He thinks, *Why not me?* instead of *Please, not me.*

Many guys display confidence in the classroom or on the playing field, but that confidence disappears when they get around girls. They go to ask a girl to the movies and end up sounding like a bumbling third grader.

"Hey, Jenny, uh, I'm bothered to sorry you. I mean, I'm sorry to bother you, but I was wondering if you saw the new superhero movie. I haven't, and I want to go . . . with you, I mean. I know it's probably a stupid movie and you might not like comic books, because most girls don't. So you don't have to go. Anyway, thanks."

That jumble of words would be right at home in the Google search results for "how not to ask a girl to the movies," because it doesn't show confidence. When you ask a girl out, have a plan. Know what you want to do and when you want to do it. Give her the facts, and ask her straight out if she wants to go with you.

And if she says no, don't let that hurt your confidence. True confidence comes from knowing God . . . and knowing that he'll never reject you.

WORD OF TRUTH

We can say with confidence, "The Lord is my helper, so I will have no fear. What can mere people do to me?"
HEBREWS 13:6

You've Got Personality!

People aren't all the same. We respond, act, and communicate in different ways. That's because we have different personalities that reflect different qualities of God. It was that way in the Bible, and it's true today. God was shaping our personalities even as we grew inside our moms.

By discovering our dominant personality and learning about other personality types, we can better understand ourselves and people around us. Check out these famous people from the Bible to discover your personality. Then build on your strengths, identify your weaknesses, and become an even better communicator and friend.

1. Life-of-the-Party Peter and Parade-Leading Miriam

Pete sometimes put his foot in his mouth (see Matthew 26:69-75). But he always bounced back after failure (see John 21:7-9), spoke powerfully (see Acts 2:14-41), and took risks to be with Jesus (see Matthew 14:28-33). He's the type of person who loved a party, oozed enthusiasm, and wanted to be the center of attention.

He was a one-person thrill ride that never stopped. He was happy, friendly, and emotional.

Miriam rejoiced loudly with a parade (see Exodus 15:20-21), but she also wanted to grab attention when she gossiped about Moses (see Numbers 12:1-2). God put her in her place (see Numbers 12:4-9). But Miriam is best known for having the courage to speak to the Egyptian princess and set her mother up as the nursemaid for Moses (see Exodus 2:7).

If you think, *That's so me!*, then you are what's called a popular sanguine. Use your enthusiasm to cheer people up and bring them together. Watch out for hogging the conversation and not following through on promises.

2. Get-'Er-Done Martha and Charge-Ahead Paul

Like Martha and the apostle Paul, do you find yourself wanting to take charge and be in control? Martha even tried to boss Jesus around (see Luke 10:38-42). She managed her brother's household and liked to invite friends over and welcome people into her home. Paul set a goal to take the truth of Christ to the known world—and did it. He took the lead in evangelism with his missionary trips. His list of accomplishments seemed endless. He established churches, wrote at least thirteen books in the New Testament, and persisted in spite of bullies, beatings, prison, and shipwrecks.

But he wasn't perfect. Paul turned away a helper who fell short of his expectations, and he tended to say things that upset people (see Acts 15:36-40). And Martha worked hard to accomplish goals and make a good impression but failed to spend time with Jesus.

Are you a natural leader with lots of ideas? Do you follow through on goals and expect others to follow you? You may be like Paul or Martha, and that's great. You're a powerful choleric. Lead on, but appreciate those who follow, avoid being bossy, and remember to say thank you.

3. The Persistence of Moses and Kindness of Tabitha

Moses complained (at first) to God, but loyally followed orders. He led God's people out of slavery in spite of his fears. He took care of the details as more than one million people followed him into the desert. He sometimes got gloomy. But he was careful, thoughtful, compassionate, and diligent (see Hebrews 11:24-29).

Tabitha was praised for her kindness (see Acts 9:36-43). She faithfully served behind the scenes, sewing clothes for people in need. She seemed to prefer not to be noticed.

If that sums you up, then you're a perfect melancholic. You may be artistic or musical. And you probably prefer hanging out in a small group or just talking one-on-one. People appreciate your loyalty, but you might need to speak up and share more. Avoid trying to be perfect, and keep on listening.

4. **Oh, Abraham and In-the-Moment Mary**

Abraham tended to be diplomatic. He was a peacekeeper in a group (see Genesis 13:7-9). But he could also procrastinate and seem lazy. Once he had a goal in mind, he worked to achieve it, and his peacemaking often involved food. Mary quietly sat and listened to Jesus (see Luke 10:39). She didn't worry about getting things done, but she enjoyed the moment.

If that reflects your personality, then you're a consistent phlegmatic. You can help keep the peace, but remember to stand up for your faith, principles, and beliefs. Use your humor kindly, without the sarcasm. Get beyond your tendency to procrastinate, and be a doer.

Some personality types click easily. Others tend to butt heads. Sometimes sanguine Peter thought choleric Paul was too aggressive. Similarly, sanguines and melancholics thrive in different social situations. Sanguines want to party, while melancholics may prefer to read.

Where do you see yourself? How about your friends?

Use these tips by personality type to talk with the opposite sex:

1. As a popular sanguine, you probably have little trouble starting a conversation. But make sure to follow through on what you say, or a guy/girl might think you are shallow and flaky.
2. Powerful cholerics love to give orders and act like experts. Try to ease up and be a good friend. Suggest things instead of commanding. Be polite. Express approval if you appreciate what a guy/girl does.
3. If you're a perfect melancholic, you probably need to relax and worry less around the opposite sex. They won't bite. Try not to shrink away or be overwhelmed by large groups. Ask questions, since you are a good listener.
4. Consistent phlegmatics can be funny. Guys and girls enjoy a good sense of humor, so let your wit show, but avoid being sarcastic. Speaking of avoidance, take action and don't procrastinate.

WORD OF TRUTH

Explore me, O God, and know the real me. Dig deeply and discover who I am. Put me to the test and watch how I handle the strain.
PSALM 139:23, THE VOICE

God's Grading System

Getting a report card can be scary, especially in your toughest subject area. But when God gives you a grade, there are no surprises. He's always handing out As.

APPROVAL
You also were included in Christ when you heard the message of truth, the gospel of your salvation. When you believed, you were marked in him with a seal, the promised Holy Spirit.
EPHESIANS 1:13, NIV

AFFECTION
Long ago the LORD said to Israel: "I have loved you, my people, with an everlasting love. With unfailing love I have drawn you to myself."
JEREMIAH 31:3

ASSURANCE
I tell you the truth, those who listen to my message and believe in God who sent me have eternal life. They will never be condemned for their sins, but they have already passed from death into life.
JOHN 5:24

ACCEPTANCE
God shows no favoritism. In every nation he accepts those who fear him and do what is right.
ACTS 10:34-35

ATTENTION

The LORD himself watches over you! The LORD stands beside you as your protective shade.

PSALM 121:5

AFFIRMATION

Since we are his children, we are his heirs. In fact, together with Christ we are heirs of God's glory. But if we are to share his glory, we must also share his suffering.

ROMANS 8:17

That's a lot of As. But God isn't an easy grader. He also gives everybody who believes in him one big, fat F.

FORGIVENESS

We praise God for the glorious grace he has poured out on us who belong to his dear Son. He is so rich in kindness and grace that he purchased our freedom with the blood of his Son and forgave our sins.

EPHESIANS 1:6-7

If you're ever bummed out by a grade you get in school, remember God's grading system. Memorize a few of these verses that speak to you. You may even want to write them on notes and pass them to friends who need encouragement.

WORD OF TRUTH

You are a chosen people. You are royal priests, a holy nation, God's very own possession. As a result, you can show others the goodness of God, for he called you out of the darkness into his wonderful light.

1 PETER 2:9

Marching Odors

Jimmy ruled the basketball locker room. And it wasn't because of his play on the court.

Jimmy was a decent athlete, but what really stood out was his hustle. He dove for loose balls on the floor. He sprinted back on defense. When his team ran conditioning drills, he always tried to come in first. He left practice a sweaty mess, which is where he showed his true prowess.

Jimmy's sweat-soaked practice jersey would turn into a type of salty "sculpture" when it dried overnight. At the next day's practice, he'd open his locker and find his jersey standing on its own. Instead of slumping into a pile like a shirt should, Jimmy's crusty practice jersey stood straight and tall. Did he ever wash it? No way! His smelly practice jersey made him a legend.

Jimmy's teammates revered him. The female team managers reviled him. While his jersey could stand on its own, these girls wished it would walk away by itself, because it smelled so bad.

Girls definitely aren't into ripe jerseys. Bad odors repel them. They want a guy who smells and looks good.

God's Word says we communicate with our aroma. Our lives "smell" a certain way to those who believe in God and those who don't. Make sure your life is telling girls that you're a guy worth getting to know.

There's no "spiritual deodorant," so we need to develop a good smell by consistently seeking after God. When we talk about God and tell people what he's doing in our lives, it's like splashing on some Holy Spirit cologne. Our actions, words, and expressions make us pleasant to be around. Kindness and boldness may not give off a physical scent, but they certainly "smell" good to a girl.

Be aware of the spiritual aroma you're giving off. A good fragrance is something worth striving for—around God and around girls. So give your bad odors their marching orders. Sorry, Jimmy.

WORD OF TRUTH

Our lives are a Christ-like fragrance rising up to God. But this fragrance is perceived differently by those who are being saved and by those who are perishing.
2 CORINTHIANS 2:15

Rightful Judge

Have you ever thrown a boomerang? If you do it right, it whizzes through the air, takes a turn, and comes back to you. It's a great trick for something that looks like a bent stick.

Sometimes you want things to come back to you like a boomerang. Other times your words and actions can boomerang back at you in a bad way. That's why it's a good idea to avoid negative words. They often boomerang back with stinging results.

We might not think anything about saying,

- "He's such a geek."
- "That guy brags too much."
- "I can't be his lab partner; he stinks."

And yet we'd be upset if we heard guys talking that way about us:

- "She's such a snob."
- "She thinks she's so smart."
- "She's not really pretty."

It's in our nature to take a quick look at someone and rush to size him or her up. But when we do that, it's not a complete picture. We may see certain attributes and behaviors, but we miss the real person. Crossing someone off our list because of a quick judgment narrows our circle of friends and keeps us from getting to know great people. Plus, we might get a reputation as someone who's critical and judgmental.

At the same time, it's okay to stand for our convictions about certain behaviors and sin. We're called to discern right from wrong (see Psalm 119:66) and do what is acceptable to God. We can show people respect while choosing to not join them in their behaviors.

Remember that God created every person. He wants us to love others and let him be the judge. God looks beyond appearances and actions and sees the heart of the person. That's something we can't do.

We can, however, watch what we say and be smart about the judgments we make. Then we won't have to worry about those "boomerang" judgments coming back to haunt us.

WORD OF TRUTH

Do not judge others, and you will not be judged. Do not condemn others, or it will all come back against you. Forgive others, and you will be forgiven.
LUKE 6:37

"I'll Be the Judge of That"

We don't walk around wearing long black robes and carrying gavels, but that doesn't mean we're not judging the people around us. We judge the way they talk, the shoes they wear, how much they weigh, and numerous other details.

The comments that come out of our mouths can sometimes make even the meanest reality TV stars sound nice by comparison.

- "Caden's not as smart as I am. He must've cheated to get the best grade in class."
- "Lucas talks weird. I can't believe Ashley's going out with him."
- "Jack can barely walk and chew gum at the same time. There's no way he deserved to make the soccer team."

While it may be impossible to entirely quit judging others, we should be aware of when and why we do it. What's the motivation behind our judgments? If we put others down to make ourselves appear better, that's a problem.

Actually, when we judge others, it almost always causes problems. That's why Jesus said, "Do not judge." Judgment is God's job. He's the only one with the wisdom to do it without sinning. When we try, we often find the speck in somebody else's eye and miss the log in our own (see Matthew 7:3). Or we make judgments based on our limited knowledge without understanding the whole story.

Because we can't totally stop judging, we should try to turn our judgments into positives. If you find yourself thinking, *That guy's a dork. He's so clueless that he'll never make friends with a girl*, then don't share your thought with anybody. Instead, encourage the guy to dress better, take regular showers, and use deodorant. We may also see guys making destructive choices by using drugs and drinking alcohol. Then we should use our good judgment to avoid those guys—and their behaviors.

By reserving our judgments and using God's standard to judge, we can honor the ultimate Judge.

WORD OF TRUTH

Do not judge others, and you will not be judged.

MATTHEW 7:1

R.I.P.

Taking a walk through the friendship cemetery can make us think. Check out these epitaphs:

> *Here lies a girl with loosened lips;*
> *She loved to hear herself talk.*
> *But because she never listened,*
> *All her friends decided to walk.*

Reminder: Stop talking and listen up.

> *Here lies a girl who never tried*
> *To learn communication.*
> *She didn't know relationships*
> *Are built on conversation.*

Reminder: Tune up your communication skills.

> *Here lies a girl who showed her wealth*
> *With gadgets and clothes galore.*
> *Alas, she was ungenerous,*
> *So she doesn't have friends anymore.*

Reminder: Make sure friends matter more than stuff.

> *Here lies a group of fun-loving girls:*
> *Creative and energetic, too.*
> *These BFFs clicked together*
> *So tight no one else could get through.*

Reminder: Widen your circle of friends.

Here lies a smart and sassy girl
Who used sarcasm to joke.
Disregard for the feelings of others
Caused her friendships to wither and croak.

Reminder: Be kind.

Here lies a terribly self-absorbed girl
Who loved to discuss Number One.
Sadly for her, all the people she met
Didn't find that subject much fun.

Reminder: Don't talk only about yourself.

Do the words on these gravestones remind you of anybody? Maybe it's you. Maybe it's a close friend with an annoying habit. We all have quirks and habits that need to be worked on.

If you see yourself in any of these epitaphs, don't worry. Examining ourselves is part of healthy living. God gives us the ability to change. And he's always helping us to change to become more like him.

WORD OF TRUTH

Examine yourselves to see if your faith is genuine. Test yourselves.
2 CORINTHIANS 13:5

Guy talk

Time for an Upgrade

Change. Some really smart people have said change is the only constant. Think about that for a minute. Change *is* inevitable (except for God, who never changes). We will change . . . for better or for worse.

James, the brother of Jesus, provides us with a great formula for godly change. He says to rid ourselves of filth and evil and replace these with truth from God's Word. Think back on the last year. What changes have you seen in your life? They could be physical changes, relationship changes, spiritual changes, or geographic changes.

Write down the changes you can think of—both positive and negative.

_____

_____

_____

_____

_____

_____

_____

Wouldn't it be nice to always have more positive changes than negative ones? We can, but it takes planning and living with purpose. Many guys would like to build their biceps, dig into their Bibles, spend time with friends, make the sports team, or get good grades. To achieve those goals, we may have to make some changes in our choices and habits.

Think about technology. It's always changing—getting better, faster, smaller, and more powerful. But it takes a lot of people working really hard to create those changes. The first cell phone weighed more than two pounds, cost almost $4,000, and could barely make phone calls. Carrying today's smartphone is like walking around with a mini-supercomputer in your pocket. That's a good change.

Just like smartphones get frequent upgrades, we should look to upgrade ourselves. Think about the following improvements:

- Rebooting our brains by filling them with God's Word.
- Upgrading our bodies by committing to sleeping more, eating right, and exercising consistently.
- Rebuilding relationships that have been damaged.
- Getting rid of any bad habits that prevent us from being the men God created us to be.

As we fill our lives with the Word of God and live out his commandments, we naturally rid ourselves of evil. That's a positive upgrade . . . a change for the better.

WORD OF TRUTH

Get rid of all the filth and evil in your lives, and humbly accept the word God has planted in your hearts, for it has the power to save your souls.

JAMES 1:21

Tongue-Tied

"People say I'm quiet."

"When I'm around a bunch of people, I want to run and hide."

Do those statements describe you? According to statistics, there's a fifty-fifty chance they do. About 50 percent of people come up as introverted on personality tests, and introverts tend to be shy.

So if you're shy, you're not alone.

If you're shy, you might feel awkward around lots of people, especially guys. But being shy doesn't mean you can't have strong relationships.

Moses was a great leader and was loved by millions of Israelites. But when God called him, Moses was shy. He didn't want to become a spokesperson, because he didn't talk well (see Exodus 4:10). God reminded Moses who had the power and who was in charge. The Lord even sent Moses' brother, Aaron, who was a much better public speaker, to help him out.

Eventually, Moses' confidence grew—and so did his faith. He learned to overcome his shyness and speak boldly before God's people and his enemies. Moses went from hanging out with sheep to leading a nation.

If shyness is getting in the way of your relationships, take steps to overcome your anxiety:

- Practice is key. Think of a few things to say or questions to ask before you enter a social situation.
- Know that you are lovable and have important thoughts.

- Use your strengths. If you are better at writing than speaking, write notes to pass out to friends, including guys.
- Speak up when opportunities arise, such as saying thanks or asking someone to pass something.
- Find a friend who will encourage you and listen when you speak.

God created you to be in a community. Don't hide from words. Trust the Word and ask God to help you grow more confident around other people.

WORD OF TRUTH

Moses pleaded with the LORD, "O Lord, I'm not very good with words. I never have been, and I'm not now, even though you have spoken to me. I get tongue-tied, and my words get tangled."

EXODUS 4:10

Guy talk

What a Character!

What do girls look for in a guy?

Cracking open the answer to that question can seem as difficult as solving a differential equation in calculus. By looking at popular Hollywood types, you might think the answer is great hair, eight-pack abs, cool clothes, and mesmerizing eyes. Those characteristics may be attractive to girls, but they all deal with the exterior. Image isn't everything. After all, you wouldn't buy a car based solely on its appearance. You'd pop the hood or drive it around—or take it to a mechanic—to make sure the car had the guts to go the distance. Girls are the same way when it comes to guys. They're more concerned with what's under our hoods.

An international teen magazine surveyed girls on what character qualities are most important to them. Take a look at this list of top answers and put a check next to the qualities you already possess.

☐ Honesty
☐ Sense of humor
☐ Friendly
☐ Sensitive
☐ Strong faith
☐ Confident
☐ Loyal
☐ Caring
☐ Stands up for beliefs
☐ Trustworthy
☐ Good listener

How did you do? If you couldn't check one of these boxes, look for ways to grow in that area. Many of these traits could be summed up in one word: *integrity*. The Bible talks a lot about integrity. In Proverbs, it says, "The integrity of the upright guides them" (11:3, ESV).

A man of integrity is the same person with his friends, by himself, and with a girl. He doesn't change. He knows who and whose he is. He's honest and sincere, and he stands up for his beliefs.

When you act with integrity, you'll attract the right kind of girl—one who'll appreciate you for who you are on the inside, not just for the way you look.

WORD OF TRUTH

The integrity of the upright guides them, but the crookedness of the treacherous destroys them.

PROVERBS 11:3, ESV

Girl talk) Stand under My Umbrella

"Misery loves company."

Have you heard that before? People have been saying it for hundreds of years. When we're feeling down, somehow it makes us feel better knowing that others are going through hard times too.

But wallowing in misery isn't good for anyone, so that saying should be expanded: "Misery loves company, so choose good company."

Miserable people make others miserable and can create a big pity party. God wants us to be joyful, not miserable. If we surround ourselves with positive friends, they can lift our spirits. That's why we need to choose good company.

When we're struggling with something, it can help to share the struggle with someone who's facing the same problem or a person who's just overcome that situation. Then we'll both know we're not alone, and we can support and encourage one another to endure.

That's true whether it's math homework, parents getting divorced, being dumped by a guy, dealing with bullying, or other problems. Difficulties cloud our day and our emotions. They make us feel like we're standing in a rainstorm. Instead of getting wet and dreary, look for somebody to SHARE an umbrella with.

Smile in the dark times. Talk about the problem, but also spend time discussing solutions. Try to focus on positive thoughts.

Help one another see God working. Pray for each other, and remind each other that God can use your struggles to strengthen you.

Acknowledge that things may need to change one step at a time. Be patient.

Release stress together with laughter, exercise, tears, and music.

Encourage one another with notes, words, listening, and prayer.

WORD OF TRUTH

We are in this struggle together. You have seen my struggle in the past, and you know that I am still in the midst of it.

PHILIPPIANS 1:30

Struggle for Good

Scientists say that cockroaches are one of the toughest things to kill. With a hard exoskeleton and nerves throughout their bodies, cockroaches continue to live even when their heads are cut off. That means they're even harder to kill than zombies!

While roaches are tough to kill, they're even harder to imitate.

Chuck Holton knew becoming an Army Ranger would take endurance, strength, and other special skills. He didn't imagine it would require him to act like a bug. But early in his training, Chuck found himself lying on his back with his hands and feet in the air in the "dying cockroach" position.

Try it for yourself—if you dare. The first few seconds don't feel too bad. But as the minutes tick by, the pain intensifies. Pretty soon you begin to wish that cockroaches didn't take so long to die.

After more than twenty minutes, Chuck wanted to drop his arms and legs and lie flat in the "sleeping human" position. But if he did that, he could be out of the Ranger program. Looking to his left and right, he saw a couple dozen other guys suffering through the same challenge. He knew the Army instructors were testing their mental and physical commitment to overcome pain.

Even if it's not our goal to be an elite soldier, God can use struggles in our lives to make us better men. When life gets hard, don't give up. Look to your left and right and find friends who will fight with you. Soldiers work best as a highly trained team. We can experience the same thing when we band together with Christian brothers.

Think about people in your life who have overcome hardships—a serious illness or injury, the loss of a loved one, family problems, or money issues. Perhaps you've experienced those things in your life. The Bible says great honor is given to people who endure under suffering.

As guys of God, we need to be like cockroaches. We need to have a fighting spirit and a faith that's hard to kill. In the end, we'll see God's kindness and mercy.

WORD OF TRUTH

We give great honor to those who endure under suffering. For instance, you know about Job, a man of great endurance. You can see how the Lord was kind to him at the end, for the Lord is full of tenderness and mercy.
JAMES 5:11

Girl talk

Distressed about Stress

Nobody likes to feel stressed out. But it's nearly impossible to avoid. School, friends, relationships, and other commitments bring their share of stress. According to the American Psychological Association (APA), about a third of teens feel overwhelmed by stress.

Stress gets a bad rap, like it's something to avoid at all costs. But some stress can be good.

- Thirst is a sign of stress that motivates us to drink something, which keeps us hydrated.
- A due date for a research paper is a source of stress that causes us to start working.
- Musical tryouts create the stress to practice and perform our best.
- Being on a team brings stress to do your best so you don't let others down.

Stress that motivates and gets us going is a positive force. It keeps us on our toes and inspires us.

The problem with stress is that it can pile up. A manageable amount of stress motivates. Too much stress paralyzes. One out of four teens say they've skipped a meal due to stress. Others say their stress level makes them depressed, tense, grumpy, or sleep deprived. And if we're grumpy and tense, we may turn our friends away when we actually need them to help us through our stress.

How stressed are you? On a ten-point scale, rate your stress (1=relaxing on a beach; 10=pulling out your hair).

1   2   3   4   5   6   7   8   9   10

Teens who took the APA survey had an average stress level of 5.8 during the school year. (Note: 3.9 is considered a healthy level of stress.)

Manage your stress by making a plan. Break down big projects into achievable steps. Put a list of responsibilities and commitments on a calendar, so you can anticipate busy times and better manage your schedule. And if you're feeling stressed, tell your friends. Doing something fun, sharing your feelings, or joking around can be great stress busters. Seek out friends who will support you and try to help you de-stress.

Look at stress as a challenge that can be overcome . . . because it can be. The Bible tells us to give God our worries, because he cares for us. We can find strength and peace in our Savior and by looking at the many blessings he gives us. So counter stress by thinking of three blessings you've received from God and three kindnesses that you've received from your friends.

Blessings from God:

1. _____

2. _____

3. _____

Kindnesses from Friends:

1. _____

2. _____

3. _____

When you're stressed, let it motivate you to pray. God wants us to cast our worries on his broad shoulders. He can carry the load and calm our spirit from all the stress that life can bring.

WORD OF TRUTH

Give all your worries and cares to God, for he cares about you.
1 PETER 5:7

Guy talk

What's Up with Worry?

Girls worry more than guys. At least, that's what researchers say. But that doesn't mean guys are worry free. We worry about our height, future, grades, safety, and the amount of hair on our chests. (Well, maybe not that last one.) We may also worry about asking a girl on a date or if she will laugh at our jokes. Answer these questions to get a take on your worry level.

True / False   1. Your gym teacher picks two captains to choose teams. You look around at your fellow classmates, worried that you may be one of the last picked.

True / False   2. You're driving home from school when your car starts to make a funny noise. You worry that it's a huge problem that's going to cost hundreds to fix.

True / False   3. Your algebra teacher hands out a unit test. You studied, but you still feel sweat forming on your forehead.

True / False   4. You finally finished your history report! Instead of feeling better, you feel worse because you're worried you'll mess up the presentation.

How'd you do? If you circled "true" most of the time, don't worry. Some worries are natural. Test anxiety and speaking in front of a group are two common worries for both guys and girls. And worrying about strange car noises can prompt us to get problems fixed before they blow up into something bigger.

The problem with worry comes when it makes our brains blurry. Worry can cloud our thinking and take up brain space. Worry can keep us from noticing others or prevent us from taking time to interact with friends. We become self-absorbed. If worries never go away or cause you to perform at a diminished level, get help from your parents, your friends, and God. Talking about our worries with a friend can make them feel less serious.

When worry has a tight grip on our lives, it can cause us to miss fun opportunities or possible cool friendships. If we're worried that we'll say something dumb, we may never talk with the new kid or the girl we like.

The Bible tells us not to worry about anything. Instead we should pray about everything. When we understand that God's in control and trust that he wants what's best for us, we don't have to worry.

Sometimes that's easier said than done. If you're a worrier, make a list of everything you worry about. Go back and look at your list. You'll probably see that many things you worry about never come true. And even if they do come true, you won't have to face them alone. So thank God for having your back, and keep praying for him to take away your worries.

WORD OF TRUTH

Don't worry about anything; instead, pray about everything. Tell God what you need, and thank him for all he has done.
PHILIPPIANS 4:6

All-Star Attitude

Growing up, Tamika Catchings was known more for her disability than her ability on the basketball court.

Her dad played in the NBA, so sports were in her blood. But she was born with hearing and speech problems. With her clunky hearing aids, big glasses, braces, and speech difficulties, Tamika was a target for bullies. Kids teased her about the way she talked and looked.

She wanted to blend in, but instead she chose to stand out . . . in sports. She worked hard so nobody could make fun of her on the court. Sports helped Tamika fit in, but God helped her feel secure.

Tamika has often said that her faith, family, and basketball made her the person she is—a fierce competitor who never gives up. Those traits helped her become a ten-time WNBA All-Star and record-breaking player for USA basketball. At the 2016 Summer Olympics, Tamika became the oldest woman to play for Team USA as she won her fourth gold medal!

Looking at Tamika's life, we can learn a lot about trusting God and overcoming obstacles. But she's also a great example of what it means to be a good sport.

- Follow the rules, without arguing with officials or coaches.
- Express appreciation for other players—win or lose.
- Encourage teammates; avoid trash-talking opponents.

Sports can teach us a lot about life: being purposeful in our training, winning with grace, handling disappointment. If you're competitive by nature, use that fire on the court and in your faith. That's what the apostle Paul did. As we read through the New Testament, we can see how competitive he was. He wanted to win and be the best, which drove him to spreading God's truth around the world.

Paul wrote a lot about sports. He talked about finishing the race and fighting the good fight (see 2 Timothy 4:7). He told Christ-followers to compete to win and to be purposeful when we play (see 1 Corinthians 9:24). Our competitive nature is God given. Our abilities and disabilities come with a purpose. When we figure that out and rely on God to improve, that's when we become all-stars.

WORD OF TRUTH

I run with purpose in every step. I am not just shadowboxing.

1 CORINTHIANS 9:26

More Than a Game

Forget about Alabama, USC, and Notre Dame. When it came to college football in the 1940s, it was hard to beat Cornell. (Okay, Alabama, USC, Michigan, and Notre Dame were pretty good back then, too. But Ivy League schools and military academies were much more competitive than they are today.)

In 1940, the Cornell Big Red were on an eighteen-game winning streak when they traveled to play Dartmouth. The Indians were struggling, but they stepped up for the big game—especially defensively.

Dartmouth held a 3–0 lead late in the fourth quarter when Cornell drove inside the Indians' ten-yard line. In the waning seconds, Cornell threw a pass for the winning touchdown. Just one problem. It was on *fifth* down. Nobody had noticed—not even the officials—that Cornell got an extra down to score.

This was before instant replay and million-dollar TV contracts. But the schools filmed the games. A day after Cornell claimed victory, both colleges' presidents were notified that the winning touchdown occurred on a play that never should've happened. After Cornell was stopped on fourth down, the ball—and the victory—should've gone to Dartmouth.

Cornell's president offered to give back the victory and make the official score 3–0. Dartmouth agreed, and the Big Red's winning streak and chance at a national championship ended.

Do you think Cornell made the right decision to give away the victory? They didn't cheat intentionally; the officials made the mistake.

Mistakes aren't made on just the playing field. What about if a cashier gives you too much change or a fast-food worker puts an extra hamburger in your bag? What would you do? It's not your fault the person made a mistake.

Cornell's president believed keeping the school's integrity was more important than a win. We all need to decide how important integrity is in our lives. Can it be bought for a hamburger?

The Bible tells us to compete to win and to finish the race. But winning doesn't always mean earthly victory. God calls us to something more—to follow Jesus on the playing field, in our relationships, at school, and in every area of our lives. And sometimes it may mean taking a "loss" to get an even bigger win.

WORD OF TRUTH

I press on to reach the end of the race and receive the heavenly prize for which God, through Christ Jesus, is calling us.
PHILIPPIANS 3:14

Girl talk Yak, Yak, YUCK!

"My bad! I shouldn't have said that."

Have words ever flown from your mouth that you wish you could take back? Maybe you've cringed when you realized that something you said wounded a friend. When we spout off in anger, the results can get ugly—fast.

Before we blame mean-spirited words on our brains being disconnected from our mouths, we need to commit to tuning in before we speak.

Danger, Danger . . .

Gossip, sarcasm, and hurtful words can be devastating. The wrong words can turn a potential friendship into a failed relationship. And if our mouths are more poisonous than toxic waste, then friends could start to avoid us. Pay attention to the signs.

Stop the anger and vengeful thoughts that cause our tongues to wag without regard for who it hurts. When anger controls our words, we'll ignore all the stop signs and do a lot of accidental damage.

Slow Down!

Like the words on the traffic sign, follow this great advice. As the Bible reminds us, be slow to get angry. Be slow to speak (especially when you are angry).

Think about how your words will affect the people close to you. Look for any danger signs before moving ahead with what you're going to say.

Do not enter certain conversations. Stay away from gossip and mean talk.

The next time you're angry, try to record what you say on your smartphone as you talk. When you're calm, listen to yourself. Notice what you said and and how you said it. Hopefully, you'll be happy with what you hear.

WORD OF TRUTH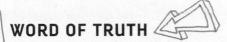

Understand this, my dear brothers and sisters: You must all be quick to listen, slow to speak, and slow to get angry. Human anger does not produce the righteousness God desires.
JAMES 1:19-20

Verbal Jousting

More than once in the Bible the tongue is called a "sword." Maybe that's why guys enjoy verbally jousting with each other. We wield our tongues like weapons as we tease and needle our friends with clever sayings like

- I've got that sweater, too, but my dog wears it.
- Your brain must feel good as new . . . because you never use it.
- I would've thrown you the ball, but I wanted to win.

Ooooh, burn! At first, teasing our friends can seem fun. It gets a laugh from other guys, and sometimes even from the friend we're putting down. Some guys think that ripping someone verbally is a way to show they accept him. *After all*, they think, *you tease the people you like to show respect.*

But have you tried this with a girl? DON'T. While teasing a girl or pulling on her pigtails may be an acceptable way to show you like her when you're in second grade, it doesn't work as you get older. Girls don't want to hang out with a quick-witted put-down artist. They want a guy who's kind and builds them up.

And the truth is, our guy friends probably feel the same way. Words can hurt, even when they're meant as a joke. So put your tongue back in the sheath behind your teeth and speak in a way that shows the true you.

The Bible tells us not to use abusive language. Instead God's Word says *our* words should be good, helpful, and encouraging. We may never make it as a stand-up comic by following this advice, but we'll definitely attract more good friends. Because both guys and girls are drawn to someone whose tongue isn't filled with barbs.

WORD OF TRUTH

Don't use foul or abusive language. Let everything you say be good and helpful, so that your words will be an encouragement to those who hear them.
EPHESIANS 4:29

Girl talk

Taming Reckless Words

You did it again. You opened your mouth and let angry, complaining, or hurtful words gush out. Did you bully someone, criticize a friend, or crush somebody's feelings?

Reckless words often start in our hearts. We lash out at others from our own pain. When we feel attacked, stressed out, or angry, our words can become poisoned darts. We shoot them with great accuracy to sting our intended marks.

The problem with words is that it's hard to take them back. Even if you later realize that you wreaked havoc on someone's day, you can't erase the impact of what you said.

We've all had to apologize and ask forgiveness for something we said. In some cases, the relationship goes on unfazed. Other times, our words cause damage that takes months—or even longer—to fully heal. While it's never too late to say we're sorry, we can't turn back the clock and make our words disappear.

Instead of finding yourself in a situation you have to apologize for, try to use your mouth for good. Be thoughtful with what you say. There's never too much kindness in the world, so choose to have a wise MOUTH. Here's how:

Make an effort to control your emotions, so you can control your tongue. Learn how to express and relieve your emotions in healthy ways.

Open your mouth only after thinking.

Use words to make a positive difference.

Touch someone with encouraging words.

Heal hurt feelings by asking for and giving forgiveness.

The Lord takes every word we say very seriously. Jesus said that one day we'll all have to answer for what we say. So make sure your words accept, not attack. Build, not bully. Cure, not criticize.

WORD OF TRUTH

I tell you, on the day of judgment people will give account for every careless word they speak.

MATTHEW 12:36, ESV

Guy talk

Thoughtful and Few

You use words every day—at school, with your friends, in conversations with your parents. Words help us express our thoughts and feelings. But sometimes words hinder communication and damage relationships. What kind of words hurt a situation? Check all boxes that apply.

☐ Sarcastic words
☐ Mean words
☐ Teasing words
☐ Thoughtless words
☐ Too many words

Did you check every box? You should have.

Thousands of years ago, King Solomon asked God for wisdom, and God delivered. Many of his wise sayings are recorded in the book of Proverbs. Solomon covers many areas of life in his writings, but he spends a substantial amount of time focused on what we say. Here are a couple of examples:

- Proverbs 10:19: "Too much talk leads to sin. Be sensible and keep your mouth shut."
- Proverbs 18:2: "Fools have no interest in understanding; they only want to air their own opinions."

Time and time again, Solomon seems to be telling us that if we like hearing ourselves talk, trouble is sure to follow. (That's pretty much what he's saying in Proverbs 29:20, too.)

When it comes to using words effectively, it's often important to keep your mouth closed and your ears open, especially when situations get emotional. This simple, four-point plan can help:

☐ Stop   ☐ Listen   ☐ Think   ☐ Speak

And if you want to be really good with words, add an additional step in the middle: pray. Ask God to help your words to be well chosen and filled with understanding. Because words are so powerful and important, your words should be thoughtful and few.

WORD OF TRUTH

There is more hope for a fool than for someone who speaks without thinking.
PROVERBS 29:20

Problems with Porn

for Guys & Girls

It can start with a simple pop-up window. One click and a pornographic image burns into your brain.

In our digitally connected world, pornography is nearly impossible to escape. You can still find it in the "old" media of TV, DVDs, and magazines, but with smartphones and iPads, laptops and Xboxes, inappropriate images are now everywhere.

The statistics are staggering. Every second nearly thirty thousand Internet users are viewing porn. Most of those are guys, but not all. Studies show that more and more girls are getting hooked on porn too. By college, 87 percent of guys and 31 percent of girls are viewing pornography on a regular basis. One in five teens say they've sent or posted naked or seminude photos of themselves. While these images are meant only for a boyfriend or girlfriend, they often get passed around.

Porn and sexting are so common that many teens think it's no big deal. In fact, some say littering is worse than looking at porn.

Here's the truth: both are trash. But litter can be easily picked up and thrown away. Porn is much, much harder to get rid of.

The problems with pornography are numerous and well documented. It's selfish. Our sexuality is supposed to be self*less*—something we share only with our spouse. Porn makes it a selfish act, dehumanizing the object of our lust. It distorts our view of the body and sex. It cheapens God's gift of sex and gives us unrealistic expectations about how people should look and act. Plus, it's addictive.

Researchers have done brain scans that show addiction to

pornography is nearly identical to alcohol or heroin addiction. And this addiction carries similar consequences:

- Building up a tolerance, so you have to consume more and more to get the same feeling
- Compulsive behavior—losing control over your actions
- Difficulty forming normal relationships
- Withdrawal symptoms when you stop

If you have a pornography problem, don't try to hide it. There's hope! Talk to a parent, a pastor, or another trusted adult. Commit to finding pleasure in your everyday life, not in images on the Internet. Focus your eyes on what is pure in God's sight— beautiful smiles, nature, and healthy food. Surround yourself with guys and girls who will encourage you . . . and do the same in their lives. Ask your parents to install accountability software and blocking programs on your phone and computer to make porn harder to access.

As with all serious addictions, don't be afraid to seek professional counseling. Defeating porn isn't something we can do on our own. We can't hide it and hope it will get better or that the desire will go away. But with dedication and hard work, a pornography problem can be overcome.

And don't forget the power of prayer. God is ready to forgive any past sin and help cleanse our minds.

When Jesus gave his famous Sermon on the Mount, he said, "If your eye—even your good eye—causes you to lust, gouge it out and throw it away. It is better for you to lose one part of your body than for your whole body to be thrown into hell" (Matthew 5:29). That sounds pretty harsh. But the Lord wasn't encouraging

self-mutilation. He was simply saying that it's better to lose part of your body than have your life ruled by sin.

Pornography can rule—and ruin—our lives and our relationships. Don't let it. Break pornography's grip on your life now, before the problem keeps popping up.

WORD OF TRUTH

You can't say that our bodies were made for sexual immorality. They were made for the Lord, and the Lord cares about our bodies.

1 CORINTHIANS 6:13

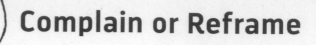

Complain or Reframe

What sounds better?

"Stay out of my room, Sis. It's rude, and you'll never have my fashion sense."

    or

"Please ask before borrowing my clothes."

"I'll do the cover since I'm better at drawing. You do the bibliography."

    or

"I can work on the cover and art, if you work on the bibliography. You're so good at details and knowing the right format."

"I'd like to hang out, but Mr. Marks is a jerk. I'll be working on his homework all night."

    or

"I'm sorry, I can't do anything tonight—too much homework. But let's try to hang out tomorrow."

It's not too hard to see which words will result in a better outcome. When we complain or criticize, it can put people on the defensive or put them in a bad mood. Here are some things to avoid:

- Avoid the blame game. Use "I" statements. So if your study buddy's explanation didn't help, say, "I still don't get it. I wonder if you can show me a different way to solve the problem." That will go over way better than, "I still don't get it. You're not very good at explaining things."
- Avoid whining by reframing your thoughts and providing helpful suggestions. If you felt ditched by a friend at school, gently mention, "I felt hurt that you raced off this morning without saying hi. Just a smile and wave would be great."
- Avoid bossing people around. Instead of telling someone what you want him or her to do, put your request in the form of a question or a suggestion that shows you are willing to share the job.

It takes practice to get along, especially without arguing or whining. That's where compromise and negotiation come in. Kindness and appreciation make a huge difference, because speaking with care gives life to the people around you.

 WORD OF TRUTH

The tongue can bring death or life; those who love to talk will reap the consequences.
PROVERBS 18:21

Gripe or Gratitude

It's so easy to complain. Your parents won't extend your curfew. The coach doesn't appreciate your talent. The music teacher won't give you the chance to play a solo. The girl you like ignores you. The teacher was too harsh grading your paper. Before you know it, your sour attitude can affect your actions. Your complaining may even affect the people around you.

Nobody likes hanging out with a complainer, so friends may start to step away. And girls may start to notice you—but for the wrong reasons.

Imagine being a business owner. You want to treat your employees right, so you pay them fairly and give annual bonuses based on their contribution to the company. Every year you give bonuses, until something hits you. *Nobody ever says "thank you." In fact,* you think, *all I hear is people complaining about how much they make, instead of talking about how much they appreciate their jobs.*

What would you do? Would you keep paying bonuses? Most of us would quit rewarding the complainers.

Complaining has consequences. Sometimes we get so caught up in circumstances that we miss the big picture. God has big plans for your life. He uses your circumstances to shape you into the man that he wants you to be.

If anybody in the Bible had reason to complain, it was Nehemiah. He went from living in a palace and being cupbearer for a king to sleeping in squalor and rebuilding a stone wall. Enemies taunted and attacked, but Nehemiah didn't complain. He stayed focused on the big picture. He knew God had given him the job to make Jerusalem safe again. Despite setbacks, Nehemiah and his workers completed the wall in just fifty-two days.

How did Nehemiah do it? The Bible says that "the people had the will to keep working" (Nehemiah 4:6, HCSB). Wall building can be monotonous, hard work. But God's people worked quickly, skillfully, and without complaining.

As God's followers, we need to be grateful for our families, teachers, coaches, and friends. Sure, all those relationships take work. But when we stop griping and work with a spirit of gratitude, it's amazing what we can accomplish.

WORD OF TRUTH

Work willingly at whatever you do, as though you were working for the Lord rather than for people.
COLOSSIANS 3:23

Girl talk

Consumed by Stuff

"Hey, is that the new tablet?"

"Did you see that Olivia got the latest smartphone?"

"Tried any new apps lately? I found a cool one."

"Abby's jeans are awesome. Do you know where she got them?"

Stuff can overtake our lives and become the only topic we talk about.

- Do you find yourself talking a lot about stuff that someone else owns?
- Are you trying to collect the most apps, reach the highest level, or build the biggest wardrobe?
- Is there a possession you think you can't live without?

Depending on how you answered those questions, you might be consumed by consumerism. It's an especially big problem in the United States, where stuff is a status symbol. The Bible warns about the problem of having too many things or being jealous of somebody else's "toys" (see Exodus 20:17; Luke 12:15).

At some point it's good for us to turn off the technology and think about the priorities in our lives. Pausing all the tech and taking time to search our hearts will help us decide what's most important in our lives. Then we can put our energy into that.

God wants to be first—actually, he demands that position. He's not interested in competing with other stuff. After all, he's the one who's ultimately responsible for giving you all the stuff you have.

If you look at your life and discover that God's not in his rightful place, make time to talk with a trusted friend. Talk with your friend about life, dreams, God, relationships, and other real topics. Notice the world and the people God created. Those are the things that matter.

Stuff breaks and becomes obsolete. But Jesus never disappoints, so invest in him.

WORD OF TRUTH

Don't love money; be satisfied with what you have. For God has said, "I will never fail you. I will never abandon you."
HEBREWS 13:5

Guy talk

Watch Your Words

Movies can contain lots of cussing. Not surprisingly, Hollywood sets can turn into swearfests as well.

Stuntman Allen "Rock" Robinson has worked in movies and TV shows for more than thirty years. With intense pressure to get an action shot and meet a deadline, he says a set can be like a high school locker room.

"Sometimes people will tell jokes or talk about things that aren't very appropriate," Allen says. "I don't stand for it, so I'll make a comment or simply walk away."

Allen has seen his words and actions have an impact. "Pretty soon people understand that there's something different," he says. "I'm not cussing like the rest of the guys or jumping in when they talk bad about somebody. I take pride in being able to stand firm in my faith while working with a lot of people."

God expects the same from all of us. Do we go along with the crowd or stand apart with our words? What we say speaks loudly about our character, especially to girls.

When adult women were asked, 74 percent of them said they are bothered by profanity. This same poll found that 54 percent of men admit to swearing at least a few times a week.

The Bible says, "Blessing and cursing come pouring out of the same mouth. Surely, my brothers and sisters, this is not right!" Instead of getting caught up in cussing, we should make sure that everything that pours from our mouths reflects our faith in Christ.

If vulgar words are part of your vocabulary, try these tips to stop using them:

- Picture your grandma standing at your shoulder, hearing everything you say.
- Set up a swear jar. Every time you cuss, throw in a dollar. When the jar is full, give the money to a homeless shelter or other good cause.
- Get your friends involved. Keep each other accountable with what you say.
- Avoid friends or situations that cause you to cuss.

When you watch your words, you honor God.

WORD OF TRUTH

Blessing and cursing come pouring out of the same mouth. Surely, my brothers and sisters, this is not right!
JAMES 3:10

Girl Talk

Photo Fail . . . and Victory

Click and post.

More than forty billion photos were posted on Instagram in its first five years of existence. A photo sent to friends can pull them into your fun. It provides a glimpse of your life and what you're doing that day.

But social media has a dark side. Photo fails can be passed around. Captions may be mocked. And with Photoshop and filters, pictures can be altered in unflattering ways. Instagram can be a bully's playground.

When it comes to social media, be wise with your posts.

- Choose who sees your photos and posts.
- Don't "friend" or follow everybody. Resist making social media into a popularity contest.
- Build relationships, and let your friends learn more about you by
  - showing a photo of you doing an activity or hobby you enjoy;
  - posting pictures of things you find beautiful or that connect you with your Creator—sunsets or other natural settings, art, etc; and
  - showing yourself studying to get a little empathy or encouragement.
- Use posts to get the word out and make a difference. Snap photos during a youth group project. Invite others to join your group.

Watch out for the following:

- Adding overlays or making edits to other people's photos. It can be funny, but also hurtful.
- Posting photos you don't want to be seen by parents, college admissions counselors, future employers, etc. Once something is posted online, it can take on a life of its own, and it's impossible to completely remove it from the Internet.

Technology is an ever-changing tool. What's cool today is gone tomorrow. But online etiquette never changes. Be kind. Be responsible. Glorify God with your posts, and always use technology for good.

WORD OF TRUTH

We are each responsible for our own conduct.
GALATIANS 6:5

Defeat Tweet

The ball was right in his hands. During overtime in a 2010 NFL game, Buffalo Bills quarterback Ryan Fitzpatrick threw a perfect pass to wide receiver Stevie Johnson in the end zone. But the normally sure-handed receiver dropped the ball. What should've been a thrilling overtime victory for the underdog Bills turned into one of the most replayed lowlights on ESPN.

After the game, Stevie, a vocal Christian and frequent Twitter user, posted this on his account: "I PRAISE YOU 24/7!!!!!! AND THIS HOW YOU DO ME!!!!! YOU EXPECT ME TO LEARN FROM THIS??? HOW???!!! ILL NEVER FORGET THIS!! EVER!!! THX THO."

Whoa! Football fans and media professionals reacted immediately to Stevie's tweet, saying he was blaming God—and not himself—for the drop. *And,* people asked themselves, *why is Stevie doing this so publicly?*

Athletes—and plenty of other people—often get themselves in trouble on Twitter. Instead of venting to a friend, they post their thoughts for millions to read. Stevie was telling the world that he'd done so much for God, but God didn't do much for him.

Do Stevie's words sound familiar? When things don't go as we had hoped, we may look to heaven and say, "Why, God?"

King David did that . . . a lot. When he was attacked or mistreated, he'd sometimes ask, "My God, my God, why have you abandoned me?"

Although crying out to God after a disappointing situation is natural, that's not where God wants the process to stop. We need to look beyond our pain to God's power and provision. That's what Stevie did the next day when he tweeted: "learned A lot Within 24hrs. Saw Both Sides.(Ups&Dwns) I AM HAPPY & THANKFUL 4 YESTERDAY! w/out Sunday iWldnt have grew closer w/The Lord!!"

Asking God *why* is okay, but it's often better to ask, "What now?" God will never abandon us. And he wants us to grow through life's difficulties—grow in faith, grow in trust, grow closer to him, and grow in wisdom—including when it comes to what we post on Twitter.

WORD OF TRUTH

My God, my God, why have you abandoned me? Why are you so far away when I groan for help?
PSALM 22:1

Knocking Down Walls

We're all wall builders. Just like people in Bible times put walls around cities, we build walls to protect ourselves.

Sometimes we close ourselves off because we've been hurt by someone in our past. To avoid more pain, we build invisible walls to prevent people from getting too close.

Maybe a guy you liked started dating your best friend. That made you so jealous that you walled yourself off and stopped talking to both of them.

Or maybe your pain is even deeper—maybe you were abused emotionally, physically, or sexually. It's completely natural for a survivor of abuse to build thick walls to protect herself.

Walls keep us safe, but they can also make us lonely. We can inadvertently imprison ourselves. When we're stuck in a cage, it's hard to grow. Our emotions and relationships get stunted. If you're trapped behind your walls, it's time to break free.

Understand that . . .

- Some people behave hurtfully; some are even abusers. But people aren't all alike. There are still trustworthy people in the world.
- You did not cause the abuse against you. Your abuser is at fault—not you.
- You can't control what other people do. But you can control how you respond to their actions.

Break down walls to build a better you by . . .

- Getting unstuffed. Hidden experiences and pain will keep hurting until you let them go. Talk to your parents or ask to meet with a Christian counselor who will help you work through your experiences.
- Letting out the tears. It's okay to grieve and be angry.
- Asking God to help you forgive those who caused the pain in your past.
- Being brave and opening up a little at a time.
- Being thankful for the people who care about you.
- Asking God to bring great people into your life.

NOTE: Breaking down walls doesn't mean that you don't have any boundaries at all. It's important to establish healthy boundaries in your relationships. Pray for discernment on who you should trust and let into your life. Your parents or another trusted adult can help with this.

WORD OF TRUTH

The LORD is close to the brokenhearted; he rescues those whose spirits are crushed.
PSALM 34:18

Guy talk

Catch a Wave

Surf's up!

Well, it is as long as you know how to catch a wave. The pros make it look easy. In truth, it takes a lot of practice and a bit of daring. As a wave approaches, you must turn toward the beach and paddle as hard as you can. The wave will then lift your surfboard higher in the water.

That's the tipping point. Your natural tendency will be to lean back, but it's important to keep your weight forward and your arms paddling. If you do it right, you'll find yourself at the highest point of the wave with a decision to make.

Do you commit to riding it, or do you bail out?

It may feel scary, but if you lean in, you'll start sliding down the face of the wave. Soon the wave will pull you in. Then all you have to do is stand up and enjoy the ride. *Cowabunga, dude!*

Catching a wave requires taking a risk. Without risk, you'll end up just bobbing up and down on your surfboard.

Life is the same way. To get the most out of it, we have to take risks. Whether it's talking to a girl we like, sharing a secret with a friend, or living out our faith in Christ, we need to be willing to take risks. Sometimes God will ask us to lean in to a situation when all we want to do is bail out. At those times, we have to trust the Lord. Psalm 84:12 reminds us that "happy is the person who trusts in You!" Keep moving forward and trusting God.

Sure, when we take risks, we sometimes will fail. That's okay. A good wipeout can be a learning experience. But to enjoy true happiness, we have to fully commit to God . . . even if it feels scary.

WORD OF TRUTH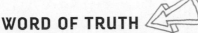

Happy is the person who trusts in You, Lord of Hosts!
PSALM 84:12, HCSB

Girl talk   Between Two Worlds

One minute guys are gross. The next minute they're still gross . . . but you kind of like them.

We live between two worlds. Part of us clings to childhood. Maybe we still have old dolls in our closet and stuffed animals on our beds. But part of us has already grown up in a lot of ways. Instead of a Mickey Mouse toothbrush, there's makeup on the bathroom counter. Every year brings more adult privileges and responsibilities.

It's the same for guys as it is for girls, except that most guys don't mature as quickly. They can't help it. Actually, none of us can control how quickly we develop. God hardwired each of our bodies, and we're on his timetable.

Researchers say teen brains don't work like adult brains— and they won't until you're in your early twenties. The parts of the brain that help you control your impulses, have good judgment, and plan strategically are among the last parts to develop.

As your brain grows and gets rewired, you need to keep asking your parents for guidance. Digging into God's Word and praying for wisdom can also help.

Science may show that girls mature faster than guys, but that's not an excuse for anybody to act immaturely.

So look for these signs of maturity in yourself and your friends:

- Ability to keep promises and commitments
- Open communication skills
- Making decisions based on facts more than on emotions

- Ability to distinguish between wants and needs
- Ability to control emotions
- Taking responsibility for actions
- Becoming less impulsive
- Becoming more patient and flexible
- Accepting negative feedback or constructive criticism as tools to improve
- Handling disappointments without whining
- Becoming gracious about winning or losing

That's a hard list to live up to. Nobody does it perfectly all the time. But as you and your friends grow, you'll put away childish things and mature into the people God has designed you to be. And it's an awesome journey.

WORD OF TRUTH

When I was a child, I spoke and thought and reasoned as a child. But when I grew up, I put away childish things.
1 CORINTHIANS 13:11

Guy talk

Why Wait?

Wait! Stop! Halt!

A lot of guys don't like hearing those words. We prefer *Go! Charge! Full speed ahead!* As men we like to take control and get things done, especially if there's a problem to be solved. It's in our blood to be a human *doing* instead of a human *being*.

But sometimes God wants us to be patient, even when there are problems to be solved.

Gideon was certainly a man with problems. The Midianites had occupied his land; they took all the crops and livestock and left little for the Israelites. Gideon's own family worshiped false gods. What's more, Gideon was *the least* in his family (see Judges 6:15).

But God called Gideon to be a mighty warrior and free his people. The Lord showed Gideon three miraculous signs. Thirty thousand guys showed up to fight with him. For most guys, that's all we'd need to shout, "Attack!" But Gideon showed faith in God by waiting for more instructions. Even when God trimmed Gideon's army to three hundred to fight a Midianite force that was "as thick as locusts," Gideon trusted God (Judges 6:5). He waited for the Lord's timing and won the battle.

When we have a need, our default response is often, *Get 'er done.* Taking action can be good, especially if we can stop our friends from making poor choices or fix something before a worse situation happens. But if we charge ahead into an especially difficult situation that we're not equipped to handle, we may cause more harm than good—to ourselves and to the people we're trying to help.

The Bible says to look to the Lord when we're in trouble. It's not easy to wait, but many times it's best to pause and pray. You'll probably never have to free your country from invaders with a handful of your friends. But when difficulties come, do the courageous thing—pray to God, be confident in him, and wait for him to lead you.

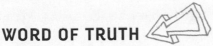

WORD OF TRUTH

As for me, I look to the Lord for help. I wait confidently for God to save me, and my God will certainly hear me.
MICAH 7:7

Grow for It

for Guys & Girls

If you could have any superpower, what would it be?

Being able to fly would make you superpopular. Invisibility would come in handy sometimes, and so would superstrength.

When Christian teens were asked what trait they wanted in a girlfriend or boyfriend, the top answer wasn't someone with claws that shot out of their hands. They just wanted someone who was serious about his or her faith.

Sadly, there's no spider bite or gamma radiation that makes us superspiritual. If we want to wield the sword of the Spirit, like Aragorn in *The Lord of the Rings*, and stop Satan's arrows with a shield of faith, it takes time and effort. Prayer, Bible reading, and getting together with other Christians is a proven winning formula. But growing in our faith happens in different ways for different people.

Take this true-or-false quiz. Which of these are ways that people in the Bible grew spiritually?

True / False   1. Getting zapped by light from above
True / False   2. Discovering a Bible that had been lost
True / False   3. Listening to a prophet tell a story
True / False   4. Paying attention to Mom and Grandma
True / False   5. Examining God's Word
True / False   6. Hearing a bird after making a bad choice
True / False   7. Listening to an older woman
True / False   8. Realizing that Jesus already knew every sin
True / False   9. Following the urging of the Holy Spirit
True / False   10. Testing God
True / False   11. Sleeping

All but the last one is true. How did you do? For extra credit, go back and write down the person in the Bible who grew closer to God in each of the first ten ways. (Answers are at the bottom of the next page.)

We can learn a lot about God by seeing how he worked in the lives of people in the Bible. He may never blind us or speak through a donkey to save us. But he can work through our different learning styles and circumstances to inspire spiritual growth.

If you feel stuck spiritually, try some of these ideas:

- Let God zap your thoughts as you read his Word. Pause while reading, and pray for him to help you understand and apply what you read.
- Start a journal. Write down favorite Bible passages that you read. Talk to God and share your thoughts. List your prayer requests.
- Listen to sermons. Most churches have a website with past sermons.
- Subscribe to Christian podcasts. Some of the best biblical teaching can be downloaded to your phone for free.
- Listen to older people and family members. Ask them to share how God has worked in their lives. See if they have any tips.
- Start a Bible study with some friends. Examine Scriptures, read commentaries, and see how God's Word applies to your life.
- When you fail at following God, turn back and ask for forgiveness. Ask him to use your past to help you be stronger and wiser in the future.
- Think of your darkest secrets. Jesus already knows what they are, and he forgives you. Thank God for always loving you.
- Practice listening for the Holy Spirit's urging. Sometimes he speaks the loudest in the quiet times.

God never stops molding us into his image. Sometimes that means we might get pinched and squashed as we grow more like him. Even when it hurts, we have to trust God in our spiritual growth.

We might not get to put out a fleece to test God like Gideon did. But know that God is open to our doubts, like he was with the apostle Thomas. It's okay to have questions. Life is full of them. And God has the answers. Search for God's truth, and he'll help you find it.

When we dig deeper into God and ask him to show us the truth, we'll see him work in our lives. As we grow in our faith, we may even become a spiritual superhero to our friends. (Note: Wearing a cape is optional.)

WORD OF TRUTH

Grow in spiritual strength and become better acquainted with our Lord and Savior Jesus Christ. To him be all glory and splendid honor, both now and forevermore.

2 PETER 3:18, TLB

Answers: 1. Paul (Acts 9); 2. Josiah (2 Kings 22:8-20); 3. David (2 Samuel 12:1-15); 4. Timothy (2 Timothy 1:5); 5. The Bereans (Acts 17:10-12); 6. Peter (Luke 22:54-62); 7. Ruth (Ruth 3); 8. The woman at the well (John 4); 9. Philip (Acts 8:26-40); 10. Gideon (Judges 6).

Broken Records

You'll never amount to anything.
Why can't you be like your sister?
You messed up again!

Do you ever replay hurtful words in your mind? Negative words that make you feel bad are hard to erase from your memory. For some reason, they play over and over in your thoughts. Sometimes people say mean things out of jealousy, anger, or spite. Other hurtful words come from another person's pain as he or she lashes out at anyone within hearing distance.

Instead of replaying cutting words, ask God to help you forgive the person who hurt you and if not completely forget the words, to at least help you put them out of your mind whenever they pop up.

Maybe you constantly replay arguments or conversations you've had, thinking about what you would've liked to do differently. You can't change the past. However, you can learn from it. So if you pick up ideas about what to do differently in the future, it's like taking a negative and turning it into a positive. Tell yourself, "I'll do better next time," and then turn your thoughts to something else.

Just like replaying negative messages in our minds can hurt us, reviewing positive statements can build us up. Positive words, like Scripture or praise songs, can brighten our moods. Memorizing and replaying Scripture are great ways to grow closer to God. Scriptures remind us that we're precious and prized in our heavenly Father's eyes.

Strangely, sometimes negative words can help and positive

words can hurt if they get stuck in your head. Compliments feel great. Accept the praise and be thankful. Let the words motivate you to continue to work hard and develop godly character traits. But be careful about replaying praise too often. You might just overinflate your ego.

On the other hand, if a teacher tells you how to improve your writing or a coach instructs you on proper technique, those are words to hold on to. Constructive criticism challenges you to change.

God gave us a lot of words to help us grow and follow him. Those are the best ones to remember.

WORD OF TRUTH

Pleasant words are a honeycomb, sweet to the soul and healing to the bones.

PROVERBS 16:24, NASB

Hitting Replay

What are you most likely to think in these situations?

1. You only do five push-ups in gym class before collapsing on the floor.
   a. *I really need to work out more.*
   b. *I'm a worthless ball of goo.*

2. You scream like a little girl when you see a mouse scamper across the school hallway.
   a. *A lot of people are afraid of mice.*
   b. *What a wimpy scaredy-cat!*

3. You sit at a lunch table, but nobody joins you.
   a. *All my friends must be really busy today.*
   b. *Who would want to hang out with a loser like me?*

If you answered *b* more often than *a*, then you may be suffering from negative self-talk.

We all have voices in our heads—the stuff our parents say, words from a coach or pastor, putdowns from a bully, and good stuff we've read. If you have more negative messages going through your head than positive ones, it's time to make a switch. Negative thoughts will come, but God's positive thoughts should rule.

The next time you start hearing negative thoughts, ask yourself, *What would my best friend say about me?* Even better, focus on what your Best Friend has already said by memorizing these pieces of Scripture:

- When you think, *I'm not smart enough.*

  Remember: "Fear of the LORD is the foundation of true knowledge" (Proverbs 1:7).

- When you think, *I'm not strong enough.*

  Remember: "I take pleasure in my weaknesses, and in the insults, hardships, persecutions, and troubles that I suffer for Christ. For when I am weak, then I am strong" (2 Corinthians 12:10).

- When you think, *I'm alone and unpopular.*

  Remember it might be a call to pray: "Jesus often withdrew to the wilderness for prayer" (Luke 5:16).

You may not possess all the qualities you want right now. But take heart. There's plenty of time to work on your weaknesses. Don't listen to negative thoughts that pop into your brain. Faithfully follow the Lord, and he'll help you stay positive.

WORD OF TRUTH

You will keep in perfect peace all who trust in you, all whose thoughts are fixed on you!
ISAIAH 26:3

Go for True Beauty

Name the celebrity you think is the most beautiful. Do you compare yourself to her constantly?

Do you look at fashion photos and notice only "perfect" body shapes and faces?

Do you stare into the mirror and cringe?

You're not alone.

Seventy percent of girls believe they don't look good enough or don't like their appearance. When we compare ourselves to models whose photos have been altered and enhanced, we're going to come up short.

So **stop** comparing yourself, and **go** for real health and inner beauty that lasts.

- Go for walks to help you be healthy and release endorphins that make you feel better and relieve stress. Use the time to pray or text a friend.
- Go for drinking water. It hydrates your skin cells to make you glow. Water can also help you maintain a healthy weight, and it keeps you healthy by lowering stress, lubricating your joints, and helping your body get rid of toxins.
- Go fill your heart with beauty as you read the Bible. Notice how God views you as beautiful.
- Go and have your photo taken with friends. Joke, smile, and laugh. Post those smiles on social media or on your walls or locker as reminders of lasting beauty and friendship.

- Go to bed on time. Sleep helps you revitalize. That's why it's called beauty rest!
- Go and dream of what you can be and what God has called you to be. There's beauty in following God's plan for your life.
- Go and eat healthily. Fill your body with nutritious foods so your skin will be healthy and you'll have plenty of energy.
- Go and pray for God to reveal the beauty he sees in you.
- Go for spiritual tips over beauty tips to become an amazing woman of faith.
- Go and admire the beauty you find in your mom, girlfriends, family members, and other real women. Notice their kindness, generosity, and loving hearts.

True beauty goes deep. It lasts and doesn't fade with age. As you develop your beauty habits, remember to also work toward becoming a woman of virtue.

WORD OF TRUTH

You should clothe yourselves instead with the beauty that comes from within, the unfading beauty of a gentle and quiet spirit, which is so precious to God.
1 PETER 3:4

Guy talk

Weight for It

We don't like to admit it. But studies show guys think about their body image almost as much as girls do. Most of us wouldn't mind being built like a professional athlete or a Hollywood action star.

Building muscle doesn't happen overnight. It takes consistent training to create bulging biceps and popping pecs. And some body types simply don't build muscle as quickly as others, no matter how much you work out.

Fitness experts say using machines is best for beginning weight lifters. Squats, bench presses, curls, and rows should be mixed in with non-weight-bearing activities, such as push-ups, pull-ups, and step-ups. And don't forget planks and crunches to build your core.

Working out three days a week is a great place to start. Your diet is also important. What you eat affects the way you look. Eggs, chicken, fish, and other proteins will help you build muscle. Don't go crazy with what you eat—like only eating protein or guzzling fitness shakes. Remember that extra calories turn into extra fat.

And remember, there are no shortcuts. Some guys—even professional athletes—have turned to steroids or human growth hormone (HGH) to get ripped quick. A study from several years ago found that more than 10 percent of teen guys reported using HGH at least once. But the side effects of these drugs can be scary . . . and even deadly. God made our bodies to build muscle. We have to wait and work hard to put on the right kind of weight.

Girls like strong guys, but many tend to be turned off by muscle-bound behemoths who are more into their calves than having a conversation. So stay away from risky strategies to get swol. Remember: there are different kinds of strength. Girls notice leadership, godly character, and integrity. There's no risk in building your spiritual muscle. Balance your time in the gym with time in God's Word. Find a workout buddy who will help you build your physical body *and* your spiritual self.

The Lord can give you more strength than doing a thousand reps on the bench press. When you find your strength in the Lord, he'll make you surefooted in life . . . and with the ladies.*

WORD OF TRUTH

The Sovereign Lord is my strength! He makes me as surefooted as a deer, able to tread upon the heights.
HABAKKUK 3:19

Note: Because girls are attracted to guys who have a strong faith—not because God runs a spiritual dating service.

Girl talk

What's Your Outlook?

You're at a restaurant with a glass of water filled midway to the top. You see it as

a. half-empty.
b. half-full.
c. a sign that you have a bad server.

Your answer to that question reflects your outlook on life. If you're a half-full girl, you probably take charge of a situation and tend to be optimistic. If you look at the glass as half-empty, then you may be more pessimistic and tend to let circumstances ruin your day.

Everyone has a natural bent. Many girls are quick to feel. We can swing from happy to sad during the course of a day— or a few minutes. Our first response is usually emotional, but even negative emotions can be positive. Look at those feelings as a way to help you proceed with caution, develop compassion, and be motivated to pray.

Train yourself to turn to God and trust your outcomes and future to him. This helps you look beyond a given situation and view it from an eternal perspective. Things might get better, or they might get worse, but trust that God will be with you no matter what.

Instead of whining or getting upset during difficult times, remind yourself of obstacles you've overcome in the past. Good memories remind us that the future will have great days. Without a little sadness, we can't experience true joy.

Don't connect happiness to achievement. View failure as another step toward reaching a goal. We might face tragedy, but God can bring good even out of the worst situations—though it may take us a long time to see it. Later, we can bring comfort to others. Finding the blessing in difficult circumstances isn't easy, but it's always possible.

No matter how we approach life, we can put on a little positivity—especially when it comes to relationships. Appreciate the people in your life for who they are, extend lots of grace to them, and believe the best about them . . . even when they don't fill your water glass.

WORD OF TRUTH

We know that God causes everything to work together for the good of those who love God and are called according to his purpose for them.

ROMANS 8:28

Guy talk

Focused on the Right Thing

Growing up on Chicago's west side, Davis didn't have much choice other than to join a gang. At least that's how he felt.

Davis was smart, athletic, and streetwise. When he looked around his neighborhood, he saw that the gang members drove the best cars, got the most respect, and had the hottest girls. Gangs ran his neighborhood. His stepbrother was in a gang, and so were most of his friends.

Sure, it could be dangerous, Davis thought. *But I'm too smart to get hurt or caught doing anything illegal.*

Davis quickly climbed the ranks of his gang, earning the rank of two-star general. Drugs, money, girls, and guns, Davis had it all . . . or so he thought. Then he got caught by the police and ended up behind bars at Cook County Jail.

One day, Davis heard a chaplain talk about Jesus Christ's forgiveness. He knew that Jesus was offering him a better way to live. Leaving the gang wasn't easy. He lost a lot. But he gained so much more with God, even joining a ministry that helped guide other guys out of gangs.

Jesus put Davis on a straight path. He had a future—one filled with hope, security, and love. But he also had a past filled with regrets.

Maybe you're stuck thinking about your mistakes. You may never have been part of a gang, but you've messed up big-time in other ways, and now you can't get those feelings out of your head.

The Bible says, "Anyone who puts a hand to the plow and then looks back is not fit for the Kingdom of God." To understand that verse, we have to go back to Bible times. When a man plowed a field, he picked out a point in the distance and stayed focused on it in order to plow a straight line. If he looked behind him, he'd lose his reference point and start wandering all over the field.

Our reference point is Jesus. Focus on him and plow ahead—straight and true. Don't look back. Your future is ahead of you with God.

WORD OF TRUTH

Jesus told him, "Anyone who puts a hand to the plow and then looks back is not fit for the Kingdom of God."
LUKE 9:62

Girl talk: Movie Star

If your life was made into a movie, what story would it tell?

That's the question that Christian band 1 Girl Nation (1GN) asks in its song "Cinema." Imagine that for a second. Would it be a horror film, a feel-good comedy, or a picture filled with drama? And here's an even bigger question: Could anybody watching your movie tell you're a Christian?

"That song is a constant reminder to point people to Christ," 1GN member Lauryn Taylor Bach says.

Your faith should be noticeable. Sure, it's way more comfortable to blend into the background. But a girl who stands up for her faith gets recognized. Being known as a Christian is a good thing, even if it doesn't always feel that way.

The Bible says, "A woman who fears the LORD will be greatly praised." That praise may come from your family, your friends, God, and guys. A girl who loves others and loves God stands out.

We can make our lives count for Christ by remembering this acrostic:

Commit to following Christ.
Honor your parents.
Respect others.
Involve God in your daily decisions.
Serve others.
Transform yourself.
Investigate the Scriptures.
Act with love.
Navigate life with prayer.

Being a Christian means that we show love and kindness to others, including our families. Our words lift people up. Friends see us laughing and enjoying life.

Following Christ is not about obeying a bunch of rules. It means living out our faith in a way that everybody can see, sort of like a movie.

1GN member Kayli Robinson says it's a heart check to think about her life being broadcast on a big screen. And she asks herself a question that she wants all girls to think about: "What would my movie be called?"

So what would you call your movie? Think about it and write the title here: _____

Now go make that movie. After all, you're the star.

WORD OF TRUTH

Charm is deceptive, and beauty does not last; but a woman who fears the LORD will be greatly praised.
PROVERBS 31:30

Guy talk No Average Joe

When he was a child, people recognized Joe as one of the best and brightest. His father and his first bosses thought he had it going on. He excelled through his teen years and beyond despite an unexpected move to a far-off country.

At his first job, Joe's work ethic and trustworthiness outshone those of his coworkers. He quickly rose to a leadership position. When the boss's wife falsely accused him of sexually assaulting her, Joe stayed true to his God and his beliefs. Even though he was thrown in jail, Joe didn't waver. He helped fellow prisoners, assisted the guards, and earned everybody's respect.

Eventually, the leader of the nation heard about Joe's integrity and abilities. He asked Joe to solve one of his most perplexing problems. When Joe had the answer, the king ordered Joe's release from jail. In no time at all, Joe was running the country as the king's most trusted adviser.

This not-so-average Joe (a.k.a. Joseph from Genesis 37–41) can teach us a lot about success. No matter what his role, Joe didn't despair. He always honored God. He worked hard and applied all of his God-given talents. Through his consistent desire to make his boss and others around him look good, Joe rose to a position of great power . . . it just took some time.

Do you want to make a difference in the world? You don't have to backstab and claw your way to the top. Just follow Joe's example. Be consistent in your actions and true to your faith.

Jesus provided a simple plan for success. He said to first seek

God's Kingdom. Next, he encouraged us to live righteously. By doing those two things, the Lord said he would give us everything we need.

God may not make you the leader of a nation or give you a fast car and a big house. But when you live righteously, God will bless you in the end . . . just like he did to Joe.

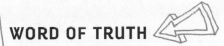

WORD OF TRUTH

Seek the Kingdom of God above all else, and live righteously, and he will give you everything you need.

MATTHEW 6:33

PART TWO

Friend Zone

If we want a friend, we have to be a friend. Obvious, right? But being a good friend isn't all about sleepovers, secrets, and shared ice-cream sundaes. Good friends motivate each other to greatness. The Bible says we should spur each other toward loving acts and good deeds (see Hebrews 10:24).

That goes for our guy friends or girl friends, who may one day become boyfriends or girlfriends.

Guys and girls often complain about being stuck in the "friend zone," especially if they like a certain person. Instead of grumbling, we should welcome the friend zone, because that's where healthy relationships begin.

Romantic relationships built solely on physical attraction and chemistry burn out. Like fireworks in the night sky, they sizzle and disappear. Long-term relationships rely on strong friendships as the fuel to keep going and healthy communication as the glue to stay connected.

This next section deals with the good, the bad, and the ugly side of friendships. It may also help you evaluate your friends (of both sexes) and decide if you want to go deeper or get away.

Girl talk

Rise above Bullies

Bullies are mean. That's kind of like saying, "The sun is hot." But it may not be obvious that bullies are also insecure and lazy. They usually attack the weak. And they build themselves up by tearing others down. The old saying is true: "Hurt people hurt people."

While guys are often attacked face-to-face, girls experience more online bullying. Every year more than two million students get harassed on social media or in text messages. Cyberbullies use false accusations, cruel statements, rumors, or ugly pictures to do their damage.

Online attacks can make your life difficult, but they're easy for the bully. A guy may start a rumor that you're a prude or that the two of you hooked up. A girl may bully you online by spewing hurtful words about your clothes, about something embarrassing you did in school, or about your personality.

If you're the victim of cyberbullying, you can combat it. Try these tips:

- Learn how to block people from your e-mail, social media, and phone. It's easier to ignore a bully if you can't see his or her attacks.
- Don't accept every friend request you get. Lots of people "friend" strangers just to inflate their friend count and make themselves look more popular, but you don't have to play that game. Only invite your real friends to see your social media pages. If you don't know somebody, don't give him or her access to your accounts.

- Never reply to any messages that are abusive or obscene. But don't delete them either. Save them and print them out if you can. Then you can show them to your parents—or the police—if things get out of hand.
- Tell your parents. They can help you figure out the best way to handle these attacks and help get inappropriate pictures or messages off other websites.

You're not helpless against bullies. Bullying, including cyberbullying, *is* against the law. Your school or the police can get involved. And God will be there to support you.

Remember who you are in Christ—not what bullies say about you. You are God's cherished child. And that's something that will never change.

WORD OF TRUTH

As many as received Him, to them He gave the right to become children of God, even to those who believe in His name.

JOHN 1:12, NASB

Guy talk

Don't Back Down

Bullies have been around since the beginning of time. Noah was bullied as he built the ark. Goliath was certainly a giant bully. Later, King Saul bullied David too. (No wonder David wrote so many "woe is me" psalms.) Nehemiah was bullied as he rebuilt the wall around Jerusalem. Even Jesus experienced bullying.

Today, bullying takes different forms. Online bullies spread rumors and hate on social networks. Cruel text messages tear you down. Plus, face-to-face bullying—both physical and verbal—still exists.

The advice the Bible gives us about bullying seems odd at first glance. Jesus said, "If someone slaps you on the right cheek, offer the other cheek also" (Matthew 5:39).

Reading those words, you might think, *Why would I want someone to hit both sides of my face?!?*

But Jesus wasn't actually encouraging his followers to let a bully continue to hurt them. To understand his words, you must know the meaning of "turning your cheek" during the time that Jesus said it.

Back then people never used their left hand to strike a person. Using the left hand was considered gross, because that hand was used for wiping yourself. (Yes, that kind of wiping.) There were no "southpaws," because everybody hit with their right hand. Bullies would nearly always use the back of their hand, because that showed superiority.

Turning your other cheek would force the bully to use the palm side of his right hand. Using the palm symbolized that the person being struck was an equal. In effect, by turning the other cheek the person being hit was saying, "I am not a victim, I am your equal." Pretty cool, huh?

Don't let bullies, guys or girls, bring you down. Stand firm. Lift your head. Let the bullies in your life know you are not willing to be a victim. Turn your cheek—or your eyes away from the screen—and walk away. Be courageous enough to ask for the help you need. That's the best way to stand up.

WORD OF TRUTH

I say, do not resist an evil person! If someone slaps you on the right cheek, offer the other cheek also.

MATTHEW 5:39

Girl talk: Guys Are Often Clueless

Do you think you can drop a hint and a guy will get it? Think again!

Guys can't read minds. Most of the time they have no idea that you're hinting at anything. Unless that "hint" is literally saying, "I'm really thirsty." When a guy hears that, he may jump up and get you something to drink—unless he gets distracted and brings back nachos instead.

A guy might really want to do something special for you on your birthday, but he might not know what you want, or he might get distracted with other things and forget the date. Instead of hinting, equip guys to succeed by telling them that your birthday is next week and you'd love it if they'd _____ (fill in the blank).

Guys also don't like to feel trapped by a question where they're not sure how to respond. If you ask, "How do you like my new haircut?" don't get upset if they say you looked fine the old way. And definitely don't get mad if they don't notice your new style—unless you just dyed your hair orange. A lot of guys miss subtle changes girls make in their appearance. If you change your look, it's better to say, "I got a new haircut, and I love it (or hate it)." Then your guy friends can sympathize or celebrate with you.

If you want to get to know a guy better, tell him. Again, some guys will never get the hint. Just say, "I'd enjoy getting to know you, and I hope we can talk more or _____ " (fill in an activity).

Save the hints for your girlfriends. Speak plainly to a guy, and he'll get your message.

Knowing our audience is important in communication. Jesus often hinted about heavenly matters when he spoke to crowds. But he also said there was a time and place to speak clearly.

Jesus was a master communicator. He knew what to say and how to say it to make his message understood. Do you get the hint?

WORD OF TRUTH

I have spoken of these matters in figures of speech, but soon I will stop speaking figuratively and will tell you plainly all about the Father.

JOHN 16:25

Stay out of the Trap

Girls don't mean to do it. They're just looking for an opinion. Well, sort of. But it feels like a trap when they turn to us and say,

"Do you like these new jeans?"

or

"What do you think of this haircut?"

or

"Have you noticed how cute Alexis looks today?"

Then they stare at us with expectant eyes, waiting to hear what we have to say. If we're at the top of our game, we may summon the wits to stammer: "Wh-what do you th-th-think?"

Most guys just look back with that deer-caught-in-the-headlights expression. Or, even worse, we fall into the trap and respond with something like "Yeah, they're okay" or "I liked your long hair better" or "Who's Alexis?"

Girls desire honesty in relationships, but they also want encouragement. Often they'll ask a question about their appearance because they want reassurance. They need a boost of confidence, and we can give it to them with a timely word.

God wants us to build each other up with our words. At the same time, our words should be honest. Saying, "It's the best haircut I've ever seen" will probably get the same irritated response from a girl as telling her that you liked her old style better.

So when you're caught by a tough question, take a breath, take your time, say a quick prayer, and give an honest and encouraging answer, like, "I think you have a great style." Then add something that you've consistently noticed about her, such as, "You also have a beautiful smile."

A nimble response like that will help you avoid any verbal "traps."

WORD OF TRUTH

Everyone enjoys a fitting reply; it is wonderful to say the right thing at the right time!
PROVERBS 15:23

Girl talk

The ABCs of Talking to Guys

Read your way through the alphabet. Mark an *S* by strengths you already possess. Put a star by the ones you most need to work on.

— **A**ppreciate the words of others. Some guys might not say a lot, so listen when they speak.

— **B**uild up others with well-chosen words. Let a guy know you notice his sense of humor, manners, athletic ability, or intelligence.

— **C**are about the guy. Ask about his schoolwork and hobbies.

— **D**iscover common interests by mentioning things you like (movies, TV shows, music, books).

— **E**ffectively use eye contact to show you're paying attention.

— **F**orgive him if he says things that annoy or hurt you. He might be feeling awkward, or maybe he doesn't know what to say.

— **G**o out of your way to smile and be friendly.

— **H**umor lightens the heart, so laugh.

— **I**ntegrity matters. Keep confidences and don't spread secrets.

— **J**oyfully sprinkle happy comments into conversations.

— **K**indness softens hearts. Ask him questions to find out which acts of kindness would mean a lot to him.

— **L**oosen up when things go wrong. Don't take yourself so seriously.

- Mean what you say. Don't flatter, play games, or make empty promises.
- Never nag a guy or use subtle hints. Say what you mean.
- Open your mind to learning more about him and his interests.
- Positive words and praise should prevail.
- Quality time shows you care.
- Respect the guy and his dreams.
- Support the guy in his goals.
- Talk about your faith. It's an important part of you.
- Use words to unite, not divide.
- Value the guy. He is precious to God!
- Weigh words carefully before speaking.
- X-ray hearing—that's active listening.
- Yearn to learn from conversations.
- Zoom in on important topics. Don't get tied up in the trivial.

WORD OF TRUTH

The tongue of the wise commends knowledge, but the mouths of fools pour out folly.

PROVERBS 15:2, ESV

Guy talk

Follow the Signs

Signs can be helpful. A church in Ohio put this message on the sign near their building: "Honk if you love Jesus. Text while driving if you want to meet Him."

That kind of advice can save your life. So could the words on this sign outside a controlled military firing area:

Danger
Military Target Area
Do Not Enter Unless Authorized
Do Not Touch Anything
It May Explode and Kill You

The messages of those signs are obvious. Other signs are harder to read . . . such as if a girl likes you. Sure, she may give off signs. She may laugh a lot when you're around. Or if you look at her, she'll be smiling. Or maybe she tosses her hair to get your attention.

But all of those signs can be tricky to read. Maybe the girl is keeping a fly away with her hair. Or she just got her braces off and wants to show off her new smile. If only girls would make it more obvious! A perfect sign would be for a girl to walk up and hand us a note:

I like you. Do you like me? Check a box: Yes ☐　　*No* ☐

As guys, we can understand that. Unfortunately, girls tend to be more subtle.

They can also change their minds. One day a girl may act like she's interested. And the next day she seems more set on your best friend.

Wouldn't it be nice if we could read girls' minds? That would make things so much easier. While we may never know exactly what's going on in a girl's head, we can know the mind of God.

When Jesus was crucified, rose from the dead, and ascended into heaven, the Father sent his Holy Spirit. With God's Spirit, we can make good decisions and better know what God wants us to do—with girls and in other areas of our lives.

By tuning in to the Holy Spirit, we can always get a clear sign. And maybe that sign will be

Danger
Not Ready for Serious Relationship with Girl
Stay in Friend Zone
Stepping Outside May Cause It to Explode

See, signs can save your life . . . and your relationships.

WORD OF TRUTH

When the Father sends the Advocate as my representative—that is, the Holy Spirit—he will teach you everything and will remind you of everything I have told you.

JOHN 14:26

Don't Mock Body Talk

Our bodies give off signals. And those signals speak louder than words. Some experts believe that more than half of what we communicate comes through body language. Only 7 percent of a message is communicated through words. Tone of voice makes up 38 percent of what people "hear." And the other 55 percent of our message comes from signals our bodies give off.

Open arms with palms facing out signal that a person is open. Arms folded across the chest or holding an object between themselves and the speaker signals a closed position.

Even the angle of the body speaks volumes. Leaning forward shows openness and agreement. Backing off shows disagreement and a desire to get away. But the part of the body that speaks the loudest is the face.

When we look at a guy's or girl's face, it's easy to get distracted by their intense eyes or long eyelashes. Perhaps we notice their full lips. But instead of being distracted by facial features, we should focus on what certain expressions tell us. What do you think these expressions mean?

1. Wide smile, wide eyes, raised eyebrows
2. Half-open eyelids, frowning lips, relaxed muscles, vacant gaze
3. One eyebrow higher than the other, pursed lips, forehead scrunched
4. Open mouth, dropped jaw, intense gaze, eyebrows raised and drawn together, wide eyes
5. Frowning lips, pouting lower lip, eyes looking down

Check your answers on the next page. If you got them all correct, you're a pro at reading facial expressions. If not, start observing people. Our eyes, nose, lips, and eyebrows all work together to send messages. Experts say we make more than twenty different facial expressions that reveal our moods. But it's not always easy to understand some of the subtle differences.

As you become a body language detective, avoid getting too carried away. If a girl has crossed arms, it could also mean "I'm cold" or "I'm feeling down." When a guy frowns or looks serious, maybe he's just hungry or his stomach hurts.

We can also be more aware of our own body language. Show that you're friendly by opening up your stance. That will help attract people and start healthy friendships.

When you get into a conversation, remember to look at a person as he or she speaks to see what they're telling you. A guy might be saying everything is okay, but his face and body say he's really having a hard time. Or maybe a girl says she wants to do something you suggest, but her expression tells you that the idea actually bores her. Take a second look at his or her face and then ask a question or suggest something else so everybody can be happy with the decision.

And don't forget the eyes. A person's eyes are a big giveaway. The Bible describes eyes as being haughty or proud in Proverbs 6:17 and 21:4. In the book of Matthew, it says the eye is the light of the body. Our eyes generally reflect our feelings. Look in the mirror when you experience various emotions, and see what your eyes are saying.

By being aware of body language and facial expressions, you can become a better friend. When we can read what a person is really feeling, we're able to give a look or say just the right word at just the right time.

for Guys & Girls

For over a hundred years, people have been saying, "A picture is worth a thousand words." A timely smile can be worth even more.

WORD OF TRUTH

When they were discouraged, I smiled at them. My look of approval was precious to them.

JOB 29:24

Silence Can Be Golden

Guys have feelings. We can't always see them, because some guys think that it isn't manly to show their emotions. But rest assured that guys are emotional beings—just like us.

Let's say you notice that a guy looks really bummed out. You ask what's wrong. Instead of saying, "Nothing," he spills his guts. Emotions flood out. Pent-up feelings gush all over you. You're overwhelmed by what he's dealing with.

What do you do?

Sometimes silence speaks the loudest.

Many guys don't use a lot of words. They appreciate silence. And guys, like girls, don't always need somebody to solve their problems. They just need a listening ear and to know somebody cares.

So if you don't know what to say to a guy, that's okay. A friendly hug, hand squeeze, or sitting beside him tells him you care.

Your presence says you support him. Your listening says, "You matter to me."

Guys can be complex. They deal with pain and disappointment in different ways. The Bible tells the story of Job. This man had everything—riches, a loving family, a great career—until God allowed all of it to be taken away. His wealth was wiped out, his kids were killed, his wife turned against him, and his health was destroyed. Job's friends gathered around him, but they didn't know what to say. His pain was too great (see Job 2:13).

After some silence, they finally started talking. You can do the same. Following a little silence, you can say, "I'm so sorry about what you're going through. I'm here."

If the guy shared a really serious problem or said he's thought about hurting himself, you can add, "I don't think I can give you all the help you need. Let's go talk with a school counselor (or a teacher, parent, or youth pastor)."

A guy doesn't always need to hear our words to know that we care. The touch of a hand can speak volumes to touch the hurt in his heart.

WORD OF TRUTH

[Job's friends] sat on the ground with him for seven days and nights. No one said a word to Job, for they saw that his suffering was too great for words.

JOB 2:13

Guy talk

Center of Attention

Here's the situation: you want to start a friendship with a certain girl. You have one class with her at school, and she goes to your church. But she acts like you're the invisible man. What do you do?

- ☐ Walk up to her in the lunchroom and demonstrate how you can stuff an entire bag of pretzels into your mouth.
- ☐ Stand near her in youth group and talk really loudly about your latest video game conquest.
- ☐ Dye your hair green and get a neck tattoo.
- ☐ Smile, say hi, and make eye contact.

While all of the options will get you noticed, only the last one will get a girl's attention in the right way. Girls don't generally appreciate macho show-offs. They don't care that you can guzzle a two-liter bottle of soda. They aren't impressed when you brag about your latest sports or video game victory. But they do notice the little things.

- ☐ Do you hold open the door for them?
- ☐ Do you say something (complimentary) when they change their hair or wear a new outfit?
- ☐ Do you pray when given the opportunity at church?
- ☐ Do you respect your parents?
- ☐ Do you treat your younger siblings nicely?

A lot of guys think they have to brag about how great they are to get a girl's attention. While there's nothing wrong with being proud of your accomplishments, girls are turned off by a braggart. King Solomon knew that, which is why he wrote, "Let someone else praise you."

If a girl becomes interested in you, she'll begin to ask questions about you. Then her friends and other people who know you can tell her what they honestly think of you (which is another reason not to be a macho show-off).

If her friend says, "He's the greatest guy in the world," it sounds a lot better than you saying, "I'm the greatest guy in the world." And that's a much better foundation for a good friendship.

WORD OF TRUTH

Let someone else praise you, not your own mouth.
PROVERBS 27:2

Talk Shop

One of the hardest parts of getting to know a guy is starting conversations. Even if you manage to begin talking, many conversations can get filled with awkward pauses. You can keep those embarrassing moments to a minimum by knowing what to say.

Like the beat of a good song, open-ended questions keep a conversation going. When you ask a question, make sure it can't be answered in a word or two . . . or with a nod or headshake. Good questions reveal something about the person you want to get to know. Try these:

- What's your favorite movie? Why?
- Where have you traveled or lived? What was interesting about the place?
- What's your favorite sport?
- What's the most interesting thing you've done recently?
- Are you an indoor or outdoor guy?
- What's your favorite animal? What do you like about it?
- How do you spend your weekends?
- What do you want to do after you graduate?
- What are three things you are thankful for?
- What are three things you like about yourself? What one thing would you like to change?
- What place would you most like to visit? What would you want to do there?
- What's the best thing about school?

- Turn a compliment into a question, like this: "I like your shoes. Do you run or play sports?"
- Mention an upcoming school or community event and ask if he plans to attend. If not, ask what he does like to attend.

Once you get an answer to a question, go a little deeper. Ask a follow-up question. After the guy responds, be prepared to share your own answer to the question.

The Bible tells us that we can "learn how to make your words what people want to hear." Communication is a learned skill. It doesn't come naturally to everybody. But it's a skill we need in order to build relationships and tell people about Jesus.

If your questions only get mumbles or one-word answers, or the guy doesn't look you in the eye, he probably doesn't want to talk. Say good-bye politely and move on to talk with someone else. If the guy smiles, responds to questions, and looks you in the eye, it could be the beginning of a good friendship and lots of conversations.

WORD OF TRUTH

Let the words you speak always be full of grace. Learn how to make your words what people want to hear. Then you will know how to answer everyone.
COLOSSIANS 4:6, NIrV

Guy talk

Something to Talk About

What did your last conversation with a girl sound like? If it went something like this, you've got to work on your game:

You: I'm so tired after playing like six hours of the latest Assassin's Creed video game last night.
Girl: So are you ready for the test?
You: Sure, I just drank a gallon of Mountain Dew, so my brain is all caffeined up. But now I have to burp like a beluga whale. *Burp!*
Girl: That's gross.
You: Mmmm, taste the Dew . . . again.

Most girls don't enjoy talking about video games or belching.

So what do they want to talk about? you might wonder.

Starting a conversation with a girl can feel a lot like trying to start a car on a cold day. We just can't get it cranking. We want our words to hum, but instead they falter and stall.

The next time you want to talk with a girl, try these ideas. Then your conversations will be attractive, just like God wants them to be.

- Ask where she got her shoes (or sweater, or backpack, etc.). People love talking about themselves. A good question can start a conversation in the right direction. Then be ready with follow-up questions. (Note: Asking, "Why do you wear your hair that way?" probably isn't the best place to start.)

- Look for common interests. Do you have the same teacher, like the same music, watch the same TV shows, or own the same smartphone? Find out what you have in common and have a discussion about why you like it best.
- Ask for help. Everybody likes to feel needed. If you're having trouble in a subject she's good at, ask for her assistance. You may end up having a great conversation and learning some study tips at the same time.
- Focus on your faith. Talk about what you're reading in the Bible, something your youth pastor said, or a cool devotional. Girls who love God want to see that you're serious about your relationship with Jesus. When it comes to a topic for conversation, God always beats gastrointestinal issues.

WORD OF TRUTH

Let your conversation be gracious and attractive so that you will have the right response for everyone.
COLOSSIANS 4:6

Girl talk

Fresh Streams of Life

Oceans remain healthy when fed by streams of clean water. In the same way, our hearts are healthier when filled by a variety of positive relationships. Check out the guys who feed into your life. Each is like a stream flowing to your heart.

Family includes your dad, brothers, uncles, grandfathers, and cousins. These guys are often the first ones who model a man's love and protection for you. Brothers might tease you, but at the heart of your relationship, they should defend and support you. Study these guys to see how they think, talk, and act. Notice what you admire in them. Enjoy the guy stuff too, like the grunts and bear hugs.

Friends include teammates, lab partners, and guys you talk to often. Some are buddies you hang out with, share interests with, and even confide in.

Church youth group provides opportunities to connect with and develop friends who share your values. Group activities take away the pressure of talking one-on-one. Doing Bible studies or taking part in various group discussions can give you insights on the male mind and help you recognize leadership qualities you admire.

Adults include teachers, pastors, coaches, and your parents' friends. Look for good role models and examples of how to communicate well. Chatting with them helps you learn to talk to men in a mature way.

Neighbors include other dads, boys, and even senior citizens. Observe the men who care for their homes and treat their families well. Comparing young boys with men helps you recognize how guys mature.

Jesus is your ultimate male role model. He laid down his life for his bride (the church) and provides rivers of life-giving water to your heart. No guy will measure up to him, but look for ones who try.

Each stream contributes something different to our lives. Some guys will be advisers and examples. Others will be friends. Still others may move to deeper relationships. But with all the guys you interact with, look for relationships that are clean and healthy.

WORD OF TRUTH

Walk in the way of good men and keep to the paths of the righteous.
PROVERBS 2:20, NASB

Wanted: Guy Friends

Guy talk

Who's your best friend? No fair saying your dog. Everybody already knows a dog is a guy's best friend.

Statistics show that most adult men can't answer that question, because many guys don't have deep friendships. Research says that one-third of guys wish they had more friends. The reasons guys don't have more real-world friends are numerous—we're loners, we're busy, we're on the computer, we don't like shopping with guys, we don't feel we need more personal interaction. But the main reason may be that we're lazy . . . at least when it comes to putting energy into our friendships.

Relationships take work. We have to listen, make time to hang out, and invest in another person's life. After going to school, working a part-time job, attending band practice, doing homework, and playing video games, many guys don't have the energy for anything else. Even if we have a lot of friends, sometimes we might ask ourselves, *Is all this work worth it?*

The answer is yes. Scientists have shown that connecting with others helps us live longer, happier lives with fewer health problems. If we lack social ties, we're more likely to be depressed. Connections come at church, at school, in Bible study, or on a sports team.

Take a moment to think of some guys you can connect with at church or in your school. Write down some ideas: _____

_____

_____

_____

The Bible tells us two people are better off than one, because they can help each other (see Ecclesiastes 4:9). So don't give up if you can't answer the question "Who's your best friend?" Keep looking. Join a new club. Try a new coffee shop. Attend a school program. Ask God to bring that person into your life.

Refuse to be a statistic, another lonely guy. Good friends are out there, and they'll help you have a healthier life.

WORD OF TRUTH

Two people are better off than one, for they can help each other succeed.

ECCLESIASTES 4:9

Girl talk

The Meaning of Respect

Girls are wired for love. We want to feel cared for. Guys like that too, but they have an inborn desire to protect and provide for their families and friends. More than love, guys are hungry for respect.

Give them RESPECT and they will appreciate you even more. Here's how:

Rejoice in a guy's success. It validates his efforts and shows your approval.

Esteem the guys in your life. Support their goals. Guys feel valued and appreciated when you ask for their help. Say thanks if they open the door for you.

Safeguard your relationship by not gossiping about or putting down a guy. Remain loyal. It gives him assurance that you care and will keep confidences.

Praise the abilities and talents you notice. Encourage a guy when he shares his dreams and when you catch him doing acts of kindness.

Effectively listen. Value his words and opinions. If a guy says he doesn't like to dance, don't nag him into dancing. He wants you to accept his comfort level.

Consider a guy's needs. He wants to be approved for what he does and who he is. If you remember and make his favorite snack, he'll know that you pay attention and care.

Trust the guy who does the right thing. He has integrity. That's the type of guy you want to get to know better. Let him know you appreciate his honor code.

WORD OF TRUTH

Respect everyone, and love the family of believers.

1 PETER 2:17

Pay Some Respect

What's the most important thing to show in a relationship with a girl?

☐ Love
☐ Affection
☐ Respect
☐ Hope
☐ Honesty

By reading the title at the top of this page, you can see that the answer is obviously *respect*. If we don't respect a girl, we may treat her badly. We could dismiss her feelings or take advantage of her. But when we respect someone, we admire who she is and want to build her up. We want to protect her reputation and honor her. That's why respect is the most important building block in a relationship.

Love is great, but love can be blind. And loving feelings can fade. Romance ebbs and flows. Respect is different. Respect is consistent and should be shown at all stages of a relationship, while deepening and growing over time. Respect increases as you see the other person as she truly is and appreciates her uniqueness (flaws and all).

If you're dating someone or even thinking about having a serious relationship with a girl, commit yourself to building your friendship on respect.

• Respect her feelings when you're having a conversation, so you don't make her feel unintelligent.

- Respect her future with your behavior, so you don't do anything that would cause her regret or emotional pain in future years.
- Respect her family by spending time with them and not doing anything that creates problems in their relationship with her.
- Respect her relationship with Christ by honoring her as a daughter of the Most High and not encouraging her to do anything that goes against her beliefs.

Respect always builds up the other person. It supports and shows value. And it's not important to just girls. Relationship experts say respect is the number-one thing guys need in a relationship. That's probably why the Bible says, "Respect everyone" (1 Peter 2:17). So forget honesty (not really), because respect *is* the best policy.

Take a few minutes to write down ways you can show respect to a girl:

_____

_____

_____

_____

_____

_____

_____

WORD OF TRUTH

Respect everyone, and love the family of believers.
1 PETER 2:17

Girl talk

Party People

What do you get when you combine people, activities, relaxing, talking, and yummy food? A party, of course!

Get-togethers with your girlfriends can be lots of fun. Hanging out together while listening to music, making food, watching movies, sharing secrets, and talking about guys can build relationships. These kinds of parties are pressure free.

But when you add guys to a party, it creates a whole different dynamic. Guys often like to push the boundaries. They'll sometimes do it at parties by bringing alcohol or daring each other to try dangerous things.

Be aware: PG parties can be lots of fun. But if that rating goes to R (or even worse), it's time to get out. One bad night can change your life forever.

Avoid problems by planning ahead. Before agreeing to attend an event, find out if adults will be around, what activities are planned, and the number of people invited. If guys are involved, make sure it's not going to be a time to pair off. Be sure to bring a phone, and call home if you need to get away. It can also be a good idea to make a contingency plan with a friend. If either of you feels uncomfortable, ditch the party and find something better to do.

Taking steps to avoid compromising situations that could result in pregnancy, underage drinking, experimenting with drugs, or other regrets is not being a goody-goody. That's just being smart.

Great parties have been going on since Bible times. In Israel, people danced, sang songs, played music, ate great food, and enjoyed themselves. God wants us to have fun. He wants us to laugh with our friends and make good memories.

If you love parties, volunteer to help plan. Play games that help girls and guys get to know each other in groups, such as capture the flag, fast charades, team scavenger hunts, or flashlight tag. Talk together. Enjoy hanging with your friends. But be safe. Going off alone with a guy or losing control of your actions can bring temptations you don't need and results you don't want.

WORD OF TRUTH

Whether you eat or drink, or whatever you do, do it all for the glory of God.
1 CORINTHIANS 10:31

Party Hero

What is a party hero?

    a. A six-foot sandwich filled with turkey, roast beef, lettuce, and tomatoes

    b. The person who pulls everybody into having fun at a party

    c. The guy who's aware if anybody's drinking too much or if a girl's in trouble

    d. All of the above

The answer is *d*.

Parties are great, but they can also bring problems. Headlines on the Internet show the dangerous side: underage drinking, illegal drug use, hooking up, fighting, or sexual abuse.

That stuff doesn't affect me, you may be thinking. *My biggest problem is eating too much of that sub.*

If that's the case, that's awesome. Keep avoiding those other temptations. But God calls us to do more. He wants us to be the kind of party heroes that keep themselves *and* others safe.

Scenario One: One of your friends has had a few drinks. It's late, and he wants to drive home. What do you do?

A party hero doesn't allow him behind the wheel—no matter what! Offer to drive. Get a group of guys together and take his keys. Even call his parents if necessary. One night of buzzed driving could end in death, for your friend or for an innocent victim.

Scenario Two: You see a guy refilling a girl's cup with spiked punch. She keeps drinking. Soon she's not in control as the guy leads her to a bedroom.

A party hero doesn't let that happen. He may walk over and say, "Hey, you promised me a dance [or a chat or to play a game]."

Being a party hero won't always make us popular. But every party needs one . . . even more than it needs a big sandwich.

God created guys to be protectors. He wants us to be on guard. The Bible says girls are weaker than us physically, but equally loved by God (see 1 Peter 3:7). Honoring and respecting girls doesn't start in marriage—it starts now. If you see a girl who's about to be taken advantage of, step up. Be courageous. Tell an adult at the party and get a bunch of other guys involved.

WORD OF TRUTH

Be on guard. Stand firm in the faith. Be courageous. Be strong.
1 CORINTHIANS 16:13

Girl talk Going Deeper

Conversations are often casual and shallow. Once in a while you go deeper in talking with a guy, and you both share from your hearts. But going deeper is a lot like peeling an onion—there are lots of layers, and it can make you cry.

It's nearly impossible to plan a really deep conversation. Somehow it happens when there's a connection and the right atmosphere. Plus, you need the time and freedom to talk. But there are elements that can help encourage deeper dialogues.

They're more likely to happen with someone who shares your faith and deep love for God. That's Christian fellowship. When brothers and sisters in Christ talk about their spiritual lives, it can create a deep connection point.

Be open to such talks by doing the following:

- Lay a foundation of trust. Show that you won't blab about everything he tells you. Demonstrate that you understand what's being said.
- Ask questions that take you deeper. Seek the whys and hopes that underlie a statement. Share significant stories that changed your life.
- Share from your heart. When you do, a guy is more likely to share from his.
- Go into what influences your thinking or inspires your goals. And always listen intently and with enthusiasm.

Read about a great conversation in Luke 24:13-32. It started with two people talking about events surrounding the death of Jesus and grew in intensity when Jesus joined them. Their hearts were bound together. As you look at that conversation, what do you notice? How did Jesus interact with these men? Write down your observations: _____

_____

_____

_____

_____

Don't settle for shallow conversations. Dare to go deeper, but also maintain boundaries. Be real friends, but don't let it lead to physical intimacy. In the end, you'll be glad you made a deep connection with your friend.

WORD OF TRUTH

What good fellowship we once enjoyed as we walked together to the house of God.

PSALM 55:14

Tell Me a Story

When Jesse and Stephanie began their friendship, they spent hours talking together. He had just moved across the country to attend college. He had a new job, new classes, new responsibilities, and new relationships.

Since the two hadn't grown up together, they wanted to learn more about each other. Talking about the weather or their favorite TV shows didn't cut it when it came to conversation. They wanted to go deeper—to figure out if their friendship could grow into a dating relationship. To cut past the surface, Jesse and Stephanie started telling each other stories:

- About their families
- About their favorite vacations
- About their high school friends
- About their experiences in high school and the activities they had been involved in
- About past relationships
- About when they accepted Christ
- About people who had influenced their lives

Before long, both of them felt like they knew the real person they were talking to. And if a conversation got quiet or they ran out of things to talk about, Stephanie would often say, "Jess, tell me a story."

Stories are powerful. They can communicate who we are and uncover important truths. Jesus knew the power of stories. Throughout his ministry, Jesus used stories to explain spiritual truths to the crowds of people who came to hear him speak. The Gospels include dozens of the stories, or parables, that Jesus used to cut to the heart of his Good News.

As you talk with girls, don't forget the power of story. Studies show that guys who are good storytellers are seen as more attractive by girls. When you start a friendship, share some of your favorite stories from growing up. Ask the girl to do the same. Stories help us go deeper than regular conversations—and illuminate important truths.

So be like Jesus and tell great stories.

WORD OF TRUTH

Jesus said, "How can I describe the Kingdom of God? What story should I use to illustrate it?"
MARK 4:30

Girl talk

Take the Lead

What would you do if you knew a friend was making bad choices? It could be shoplifting, smoking, cheating, doing drugs, dating the wrong person—anything that hurts his character or takes her down a dangerous path.

If your friend is going the wrong way, LEAD him or her in a better direction.

Listen. It's always good to listen without judging. Repeat back what you hear your friend saying to make sure you understand. Ask questions to get to the root problem that caused the poor choice.

Encourage. Let your friend know that you care about him and his future. Any poor decision can be overcome. Encourage your friend's good thoughts and ideas about getting his life back on track. Remind him of positive past choices and blessings.

Avoid giving pat answers, quoting Scripture, or telling her what to do. Don't trivialize her feelings and actions or make a joke of them. Act with love. Love is a verb, so serve your friend in little ways.

Draw out possible solutions and new choices from your friend. He needs to give control of his life to God to get on a positive path. He'll need God's strength to follow through on his choice. Offer to do positive activities that he normally enjoys to help him release stress and regain a better outlook.

Leading a friend to better decisions is a fantastic goal. The Bible wants us to provide good counsel to our friends. But we need to remember that we're not trained counselors. Know when to listen, when to advise, and when to seek outside help. Remember these tips:

- Don't become part of the problem by going along with or engaging in the bad choice.
- Be prepared for rejection. Your help may be ignored. Stay available and pray.
- If your friend is suicidal, deeply depressed, involved in a crime, or putting him- or herself in danger, go to a parent or other trusted adult for help. Saving a life is worth risking a friendship.
- As you lead your friend, don't mislead yourself. Make sure you're not getting so emotionally involved that you neglect your schoolwork, other friends, and responsibilities.

WORD OF TRUTH

Oil and perfume make the heart glad, and the sweetness of a friend comes from his earnest counsel.

PROVERBS 27:9, ESV

The Wrong Way

A friend you've known forever starts hanging out with the wrong crowd. You see it, his dog sees it, even astronauts on the International Space Station see it. This new group is pulling your friend in a bad direction. Everybody knows it . . . except your friend.

You've got a choice to make:

a. Bail on your buddy. If he wants new friends, then so do you.
b. Start hanging out with his new group of friends, trying to fit in.
c. Take your friend to coffee and have a serious conversation.
d. Tell his parents to make him hang out with you more.

Our natural response may be *a*. When we see good friends drift away, we do the same by finding new friends. Going with *b* is just asking for trouble—for yourself and your friend. You may have to eventually go with *d* (or something like it) if your friend is getting involved in something illegal or dangerous. But the best option is *c*.

If we know someone—whether it's a guy or girl—who's going the wrong way, it's our responsibility as a friend to step in and point them in the right direction. The Bible says wounds from a friend are better than kisses from an enemy (see Proverbs 27:6). God's not telling us to slap our friends upside the head. The "wounds" aren't physical. They come from tough talk.

Here are some tips:

- Find out what's going on. Most bad decisions stem from not knowing how to handle a painful situation or dealing with feelings of inadequacy. Let your friend explain the decisions he or she is making.
- Don't judge. That's God's role. Plus, it puts the person on the defensive. You should share your concerns and point to God's way.
- Admit your own failures. Maybe you let this friend down. Or perhaps you've made poor choices in the past. Nobody makes the right decision all the time. Let your friend know you're there to help any way you can.
- Commit to prayer. Pray for your friend. Pray at the end of your talk, and promise to continue to pray.

WORD OF TRUTH

Wounds from a sincere friend are better than many kisses from an enemy.
PROVERBS 27:6

Girl talk
The ABCs of Motivation

We all have self-doubt. It's true for guys, too. Sometimes we just need somebody who believes in us to help us become the person we know we should be. God can use us to motivate the guys in our lives. Start with basics, like these ABCs.

Acknowledge his feelings and dreams. Tell him you appreciate him talking with you.

Ask when you don't understand him. If he does something silly, makes weird noises, or uses terms you don't understand, ask him to explain.

Appreciate him. Thank him for his kind actions.

Attention is key. Avoid checking your phone or texting when you're talking with him.

Be a sounding board where he can share ideas, doubts, and decisions.

Believe in him. Let him know you think he'll overcome any challenge.

Confirm his talents. Point out his accomplishments or his good deeds.

Commend him to others, both to his face and when he's not around.

Consider how God sees him, and pray for God's best for him.

You can make a difference by gently motivating a guy. Good friends encourage each other to accomplish more than they thought possible.

God calls us to be his hands and feet. By "foot," sometimes God means being a listening ear. Sometimes we're his mouth as we give just the right advice. Sometimes prayer is what a friend needs.

As we think of ways to motivate our friends, don't forget to point them back to God. When we see him using us, it's the ultimate motivation.

WORD OF TRUTH

Let us think of ways to motivate one another to acts of love and good works.

HEBREWS 10:24

Guy talk

Driven to Distraction

Most places have laws against texting and driving. Maybe you've seen the statistics:

- More than 1.6 million car accidents are caused by cell phone use every year.
- Most teens say they can safely text and drive. But studies show teens distracted by technology have the reaction time of a seventy-year-old.
- Two out of ten teen drivers involved in fatal crashes are distracted by their phones.

Distracted driving can result in death. As technology grows, it's easier and easier to be distracted behind the wheel . . . and in life. Instead of focusing on the road or the people in our lives, we get sucked in by a screen. When we keep our eyes down, we can miss out on a lot.

A famous Christian singer tells the story of visiting a church youth group for the first time when she was younger. Most of the teens were involved with their friends or distracted by gadgets. She was about to blow off the whole church thing when a guy walked up to her. He introduced himself and took her around to a few of his friends. He followed up with a phone call a few days later, encouraging her to come back to church. She did, and it set her life on a whole new path.

If he'd been playing *Pokémon Go* or texting a friend, he could've missed recognizing a lonely girl who was looking for a way out of the party lifestyle.

What are you missing? Watching people walk into water fountains or bump into doors because they're focused on their phones is funny. But missing out on an opportunity to build a relationship is no laughing matter.

The apostle Paul wasn't talking about texting and driving when he wrote we should serve the Lord with as few distractions as possible. But his words are truer today than they have ever been.

When we're at school, in church, or behind the wheel, we should look up, look around, and do what we can to make a difference for God.

WORD OF TRUTH

I want you to do whatever will help you serve the Lord best, with as few distractions as possible.

1 CORINTHIANS 7:35

Girl Talk: A Friend in Need

Depression, thoughts of self-harm, and despair can overtake a person. The teen years can be filled with emotion. Bullying, cliques, and loneliness can push guys and girls to the edge. Be watchful. You may know someone who's at a dangerous crossroads.

Below are some warning signs to look for:

- Changes in behavior, like talking less
- Complaints about health
- Giving away favorite things
- Becoming more emotional, especially angry
- Loss of interest in activities
- Doing dangerous things
- Change in appetite
- Change in sleep habits
- Talking about wanting to get away
- Unhappiness
- Not caring about grooming and personal appearance
- Self-abuse
- Trouble coping with a major life change, like parents getting divorced, being cut from the team, a breakup, or rejection

If you see someone displaying these warning signs, respond with love and courage. But don't do it alone. Pull in other friends, talk to a school counselor, and let the person's parents know. There are some things you can do to help:

- Be there with your friend.
- Ask questions. Is your friend depressed? Is she thinking about harming herself?
- Listen.
- Understand and don't judge.
- Stay calm and pray.
- Discuss options about what he can do about his problems.
- Show you care as you listen, hug, and encourage.
- Help him envision new dreams and goals.

Even with all of today's technology that's supposed to connect people, many teens feel disconnected. God's Word says that someone who falls alone is in real trouble. Reach out and help the people around you. Make sure they know they're not alone.

WORD OF TRUTH

If one person falls, the other can reach out and help. But someone who falls alone is in real trouble.
ECCLESIASTES 4:10

Guy talk Friend to the Friendless

Jeremiah saw Vanessa shuffle into youth group. She'd been coming for a while, but she normally stuck to herself. Because of her so-last-year clothes, big glasses, and greasy hair, the girls kept their distance.

That's probably why the guys don't talk to her either, Jeremiah thought.

For some reason, Jeremiah thought Vanessa looked extra bummed out tonight. She trudged to the back of the room and sat down. No one else was near her. No one welcomed her.

I'm going to change that, Jeremiah thought. He walked across the room and sat down next to her.

"I'm Jeremiah," he said. "How are you?"

"I'm okay."

Jeremiah looked Vanessa in the eyes and asked, "How are you really doing?"

She gulped. "You really want to know?" she asked.

Jeremiah nodded. "I've seen you around for a while, and I'm really sorry that I haven't talked to you before."

Vanessa slumped in her chair and poured out her story. Her parents had divorced, so she'd moved here with her mom. She didn't like meeting new people and really missed her old friends.

Jeremiah told her that he admired her strength to keep coming to church when everybody ignored her.

Vanessa grasped his hand and said, "I'm not strong. I planned to run away tonight unless someone showed they cared. I'm tired of being alone."

Jeremiah prayed with Vanessa, reminding her about how much God loved her and cared for her. As he ended his prayer, the youth pastor walked up.

"How are you doing tonight, Vanessa?" he asked.

Being depressed isn't a sin. God can use us to help someone know that they're valuable—to us and to him.

We may never end up in a situation exactly like Jeremiah's. But God wants us to be on the lookout for people who might be depressed or feel left out. We can show we care by saying hi, looking the person in the eye, and listening. Our words can build up the person. Our actions can show that the person is valued. When we reach out with love, it can change somebody's life . . . and our own.

WORD OF TRUTH

Continue to show deep love for each other, for love covers a multitude of sins.

1 PETER 4:8

Listen with Love

For Guys & Girls

A friend tells you they're struggling with their gender identity or same-sex attraction. How would you react?

a. Step back in shock, gasping, "Keep away from me."
b. Hug your friend and say, "I thought so."
c. Shout, "That's a sin!" Then quote Bible verses at them.
d. Smile at your friend, thank them for trusting you, and tell them nothing will change your friendship and love for them.

With alternative lifestyles and LGBT themes appearing more and more in books, TV, and movies, we'll all eventually be faced with questions about sexual identity and orientation. Many of us may encounter people who are following or considering an alternative lifestyle. Before that happens, we need to decide how we're going to react. Our reaction could sway how our friend views Christianity and Christ.

So if a friend comes out to you, the best way to react is *d*.

Love, not judgment, is the distinguishing characteristic of the Christian faith. Jesus said the world would recognize us as his disciples by our love for one another (see John 13:35)—not our ability to spout the list of sins from Galatians 5:19-21.

Jesus demonstrated this love throughout his ministry on earth. When he saw a crowd of hungry people, he felt compassion (see Matthew 14:14). He didn't question their lifestyles or ask any of them to declare their faith in him. He fed them. He cared about them. The next day, Jesus offered them words of hope (see John 6:22-45). That's how we need to treat our friends—with caring and words of hope.

Compassion, not condemnation, will keep your friend open to what you have to say. Treat them with respect and consideration. Love them. Many people choose to turn from faith in God or make alternative choices because of past wounds from the church or a Christian they knew. Be a friend who listens and cares.

But don't do it alone. Pull in your youth pastor, parents, or other friends. Ask for their advice and prayers. Demonstrate God's love, but always point to God's standards and forgiveness.

Jesus died so every sin could be forgiven. Whether it's lying, cheating, gossiping, idolatry, or homosexuality, no sin is beyond Jesus' ability to forgive.

Remember that we don't set the standard for right and wrong. God does. He's the only perfect judge. So when the Bible says, "Do not practice homosexuality, having sex with another man as with a woman. It is a detestable sin" (Leviticus 18:22), that's exactly what it means. Homosexuality is a sin, just like envy is a sin.

Some people react so emotionally when Christians say homosexuality is a sin. But we're *all* sinners.

Nobody is above God's judgment, just like nobody is beyond God's love. Jesus didn't get into an argument or condemn the woman caught in sexual sin. He challenged the onlookers in the crowd to examine themselves. Then he said, "Let the one who has never sinned throw the first stone." When everyone left, then he told the woman to stop sinning (see John 8:1-11).

As we encounter questions about identity or sexual orientation, we should keep in mind that our maleness or femaleness is a gift from God. It's a good gift, just like our talents, creativity, intellect, and personality. And all of those gifts should be used for God's purposes.

God had a plan and purpose for making men different from women. Jesus reaffirmed this in Matthew 19:4-6. It takes a man

and a woman to create a child, because God made it that way. God creates life and loves every person.

The apostle Paul dealt with a lot of emotionally charged topics. From sexual sin to false teaching, Paul saw society and the church make a lot of decisions that didn't honor God. But he had some good advice for Christ followers when he said, "Be on guard. Stand firm in the faith. Be courageous. Be strong. And do everything with love" (1 Corinthians 16:13-14).

No matter what we encounter or what issue we have to deal with, we can hold onto Paul's words to stand firm with God, be courageous, and act with love.

And remember to pray. Pray for God to open hearts and minds. Only God can convict us of our sins and bring true healing and freedom. Prayer works wonders, even in sensitive issues.

WORD OF TRUTH

Be on guard. Stand firm in the faith. Be courageous.
Be strong. And do everything with love.

1 CORINTHIANS 16:13-14

It's Easy to Be Green

Do you look with envy on a friend who has a boyfriend? Have you ever complained to your boyfriend that he's spending too much time with his guy friends? Do you wish you had the latest iPhone or convertible like the rich kids at school?

Jealousy can start with feelings of insecurity or the desire to have more. If we allow those feelings to fester and grow, they can split relationships apart.

Take a look at Michal, David's first wife (see 2 Samuel 6:16-23). When her husband returned with the Ark of the Covenant that contained the Ten Commandments, he danced and praised God. Maybe she was upset that David didn't run to her first. Maybe she was jealous of the relationship he had with God. She certainly didn't rejoice with him or join the celebration. She looked at him and despised him. She called him shameless and vulgar. As God's appointed leader, David stood firm. He declared that he was willing to look foolish for God. In the end, Michal's attitude destroyed their relationship.

When we experience feelings of jealousy, it's hard to not react. But before we flip out, we need to think about the situation. Ask yourself what you resent about a person's behavior, attitude, or possession. What do you fear? Pray for God to heal the jealousy in your heart. These ideas can help:

- Ask God to help you forgive people you are upset with.
- Don't try to control other people.
- Change your focus to one of gratitude that God is blessing someone you care about.

- Give thanks for what you have.
- Stop comparing yourself to others.
- Look to Jesus and trust him.

Living with jealousy can make us bitter and cause us to miss out on many of God's blessings. But when we believe that Jesus will bring loyal people and good things into our lives, it'll help us realize all the blessings we already have.

WORD OF TRUTH

Jealousy and selfishness are not God's kind of wisdom. Such things are earthly, unspiritual, and demonic.

JAMES 3:15

Guy talk

Don't Tempt Me

Here's the scene: three guys changing for gym class.

Luke: Hey, I just benched 150 yesterday. Pretty soon, I'll be reppin' with that weight.

Blake: Cool. I just ran a 4:30 in the 1600. Coach thinks I'll make state.

Jackson: Well, I'm having trouble staying away from porn on the Internet. The temptation is too much.

Does that conversation ring true? Probably not. No guy brags about benching 150 (just kidding). Actually, guys rarely talk about their weaknesses. We like to brag about our strengths: our grades, the girls who like us, how many points we scored, or the decibels the sound system in our car can output. But it feels embarrassing to talk about what tempts us.

When we admit our weaknesses, it can feel like telling somebody, "My spiritual muscle is as strong as a ninety-eight-pound weakling." Instead of admitting to our friends that we're struggling, we act like we have it all together. We don't want to seem like some sicko, so we put up a strong front and struggle in silence.

Here's the truth: although we probably don't want to admit our porn problem in the locker room, we can't battle temptation alone. Every guy faces temptations, whether it's porn, pride, or another powerful appetite. We're stronger when we stand together. And we should never forget that Jesus is on our side.

The apostle Paul said as much in 1 Corinthians 10:13, and then he added, "When you are tempted, [God] will show you a way out so that you can endure." Sometimes that way out is finding a friend who you can be totally honest with and who will hold you accountable.

Temptation is everywhere. Don't think you're a wimp if you fail. Be honest about your weaknesses, tap into God's power, and remember that you can overcome.

WORD OF TRUTH

The temptations in your life are no different from what others experience. And God is faithful. He will not allow the temptation to be more than you can stand. When you are tempted, he will show you a way out so that you can endure.

1 CORINTHIANS 10:13

Girl Talk — Avoid the Explosion

Have you ever blown up a balloon and had it slip from your lips? *Ffftttttt!* Without being tied off, it hisses and whizzes around the room until all the air escapes. When it's finally empty, it plops to the ground in a deflated mess.

But what if the air didn't escape? What if you kept filling the balloon with more and more pressure? Eventually, it would pop.

Anger works a lot like that. If we let anger build up, eventually we'll explode. Our girlfriends might understand our angry bursts because they know us, and they may act the same way. But guys will probably be shocked. They often don't know how to handle a girl's varying emotions, so they retreat—fast!

Instead of exploding, it's best to release our pent-up feelings in controlled bursts and acceptable ways. The Bible says gentle words can deflect anger. If you find yourself in a heated situation, try to stay calm. Speaking harshly can add fuel to the fire. Try these ideas to help yourself or a friend keep anger under control:

- Exercise, such as jogging or working out, releases endorphins that can help you feel better.
- Don't confront anyone until you're calm.
- Pray for peace.
- Talk to a trusted friend about your feelings.
- Relax with music or a hot bath.
- Watch funny videos or read jokes that make you laugh.
- Write about your feelings in a journal or on a computer where you can erase your thoughts later.

- Breathe deeply and count to ten.
- Watch what causes your anger and avoid those triggers.
- Respond to angry people in your life with gentle words.
- Make a stress ball from a balloon. Use a funnel to fill a balloon with cornstarch or sand to about the size of your hand. Tie it off. (If you can, put the balloon inside another balloon to make it stronger.) Then squeeze it to help relieve stress, anger, and frustration.

Of course, anger isn't a problem only for girls. Watch out for angry guys. If a guy exhibits anger, take a time out. Flee a situation if you think a guy might get aggressive. If a guy ever hits you or threatens to hit you, cut off contact with him and tell a parent immediately.

WORD OF TRUTH

A gentle answer deflects anger, but harsh words make tempers flare.
PROVERBS 15:1

Guy talk) One Up

What is it about guys that we feel we have to one-up each other?

If a friend says he's a level twenty cleric, you have to point out that you're a level twenty-*one* marksman. If you hear somebody talking about his new mountain bike, you have to mention how you rented a $10,000 mountain bike on vacation and broke the speed record on a downhill course. If a friend says he kissed a girl over the summer, you have to say . . . well, you know what you'd say.

As guys we're wired to want to be bigger and better. And that can lead to bragging. Have you ever said something like this?

- ☐ I only go out with models.
- ☐ I'm so good at algebra that the teacher had to give me an advanced book.
- ☐ Coach says I'm talented enough to get a Division I scholarship.

Being proud of your accomplishments is okay. When you work hard and achieve a goal, you should be proud. But bragging crosses the line into being *prideful*, which doesn't make you look good to girls or to God.

The Bible says, "God opposes the proud but gives grace to the humble" (James 4:6). Girls feel the same way. When a guy brags, it shows he's self-focused and needs attention. Being selfish and needy are *not* traits girls look for in guys.

Humble people wait for others to lift them up. They do the right thing and work hard, because it's what God wants them to do.

The apostle Paul had a lot of accomplishments he could've bragged about. But instead, he said, "If you want to boast, boast only about the Lord" (2 Corinthians 10:17). A lot of people know that passage, but they don't know the next verse. It says, "When people commend themselves, it doesn't count for much. The important thing is for the Lord to commend them" (verse 18).

Bragging certainly doesn't count for much. But when the Lord brags about us—that's something that will truly lift us up.

WORD OF TRUTH

If you want to boast, boast only about the Lord.
2 CORINTHIANS 10:17

Avoid the Argument

You're friends with a guy, but he's not a believer in Christ.

We've all been there. Leaving the house without running into someone who opposes our beliefs is impossible. Besides, God doesn't want us to hide in a holy huddle. He wants us to get out and be his light in the world.

As we interact with different people, some will naturally ask what makes us so hopeful and joyful. Others will see our faith in how we answer a question at school or give advice to a friend.

But transforming someone's thinking doesn't come from lecturing. It's rare that we can argue someone into the Kingdom of God. So instead of debating someone about our faith, we should look for opportunities to witness by sharing how God has answered our prayers. We serve an active and loving God, so we should tell others about the difference he's made in our lives.

And because people will ask questions, make sure you know what you believe about Jesus. Be firm but loving as you explain your beliefs. And don't be afraid to ask some thought-provoking questions of your own. People want answers to life's bigger questions. A good question could start a life-changing conversation.

- Why are you here (what's your purpose)?
- How do you know right from wrong?
- When you have problems, what gets you through?
- What do you believe happens when a person dies?
- What do you think will help solve the world's problems?

Listen as your friend answers your questions. Be open to questions from him. If you're asked a tough question, admit you don't have all the answers. Promise to think about it, research it, and get back to the person later. Then spend time searching the Bible or asking a parent or pastor how they would respond.

As we live out our faith, we can pray for opportunities to talk about our relationship with Jesus. We can't avoid the difficult issues, but we can avoid arguing about them.

WORD OF TRUTH

You must worship Christ as Lord of your life. And if someone asks about your hope as a believer, always be ready to explain it.

1 PETER 3:15

Guy talk

Be a Uniter, Not a Divider

Every year at the beginning of October, hundreds of thousands of students take their Bible to school for Bring Your Bible to School Day.

A day to celebrate God is great. A year is even better. And there's no law against carrying God's Word to school every day. As long as we don't disrupt class or cause chaos, we can talk about God and read our Bibles during school. Most schools will even allow a Bible club, if it's sponsored by a teacher.

God doesn't want us to keep our faith to ourselves. He wants us to live it out in the open. If you're interested in starting a Bible club at your school, try these tips:

1. Find a Christian teacher or administrator who will sponsor your club.
2. Talk to your principal about when and where you can meet.
3. Connect with other Christians. Ask them to pray for your group and invite their friends.
4. Lobby in the lunchroom. Come up with a fun way to promote your club when people are eating in the cafeteria. Talk about your activities on social media, too.
5. Reach out. Do a canned food drive for the homeless. Collect toiletries for the needy. Care about your community's physical needs as you build up club members' spiritual needs.

Following God is nothing to be embarrassed about. Some people may make fun of your faith, but as you reach out with God's love, you'll find more friends than foes. God can use you to help change lives and bring people to him. But you have to be bold enough to take the first step.

When Matt started a Christian club at his high school, he was the only one at the first meeting. Slowly, things started to build. A youth retreat pulled in more people. Pretty soon so many guys and girls were coming that they had to start several Bible studies. By the time Matt graduated, more than one hundred students attended weekly meetings.

Sharing your faith has to start somewhere, and bringing your Bible to school is a great way to begin.

WORD OF TRUTH

I am not ashamed of this Good News about Christ. It is the power of God at work, saving everyone who believes.
ROMANS 1:16

Don't Cave In

Unless you're into spelunking, it's best to not cave. Caving can be dangerous . . .

"C'mon, you'll just get a buzz from this stuff. It's fun."

"Weed is natural. God made it. Just try it once."

The pressures to try drugs, alcohol, cigarettes, and other illegal activities can be hard to resist. If many of our friends are doing it, it can feel like we're trying to hold up the roof of a cave.

Before you cave in, try these cave-resisting tips:

- Pray for strength.
- Find a friend who will stand with you. Agree together to stay firm and not do drugs or drink alcohol.
- Respond with truth. Look the person who's pressuring you in the eye, smile, and say, "No thanks. That's against my _____" (fill in blank with: religion, values, or future I'm building).
- Pack your free time with positive activities that make you feel good: sports, music, hobbies, friends, etc.
- Be kind, and not judgmental, to people who get addicted by their behaviors.
- Avoid sticky situations, such as parties without parents or hangouts where kids are known for doing drugs or drinking alcohol.
- If someone's pressuring you, change the topic: "I like that outfit." "What did you think of the new movie?"

- Suggest alternatives. "Let's _____" (play a game, watch a movie, go shopping, update our social media accounts).
- Face your fears by answering these questions:
  - If your friends reject you, are they really the people you want to hang with?
  - Is it really worth jeopardizing your future just to avoid hurting a friend's feelings?
- Make an escape plan. If you find yourself experiencing a cave-in, signal your mom or best friend with a text that says, "HELP." Then they can call, come pick you up, or give you an excuse to leave.

God can give us an out for any situation we face. But we need to turn to him and be more concerned with what he thinks of us than our friends' judgments. When we trust God to rescue us, he'll always be there to keep us from caving in.

WORD OF TRUTH

The Lord can rescue you and me from the temptations that surround us, and continue to punish the ungodly until the day of final judgment comes.

2 PETER 2:9, TLB

Guy talk · Under Pressure

Have you ever studied the effects of pressure?

If you follow some basic safety measures (wearing protective eyewear and using pot holders), you can see the crushing power of pressure with this experiment. Just get

- an empty aluminum soda can,
- a pot of water,
- tongs or pot holders, and
- a large bowl of ice water.

You may also want to alert your parents, in case you mess up the kitchen.

Start by filling the can one-quarter full with water. Place a pot with some more water on the stove. Put the can in the pot and turn the burner on high. As the water in the can starts to boil, you'll see steam coming out of it. Turn off the stove. Keep your face away from the can as you lift it from the pot with the tongs. While holding the can above the icy water, quickly flip over the can, and submerge it upside down in the ice. Stand back and watch as pressure crushes the can.

Have you ever felt like that can—crushed by the pressure to fit in?

Here's a shocking truth: because of God's love and forgiveness, we're free. We don't need to feel any pressure to fit in, because we already have the acceptance and joy found in Jesus. It's actually the people who are trying to get us to try dangerous behaviors who are trapped.

The apostle Paul explained it best when he wrote that some people say they're allowed to do anything. That's true, sort of. Not everything is good for us, and there are laws against certain actions.

Guys who choose the party scene and get involved in drugs and alcohol soon find themselves under pressure to get the next fix. The high lasts only moments, so they need more. Even though they think they can do anything, they become slaves to what they thought would bring freedom.

That's no way to live. Avoid the pressure and live with true freedom in Christ.

WORD OF TRUTH

You say, "I am allowed to do anything"—but not everything is good for you. And even though "I am allowed to do anything," I must not become a slave to anything.
1 CORINTHIANS 6:12

Flocking Together in Harmony

for Guys & Girls

The Wright brothers watched birds to figure out how to construct the first airplane's wings. Swiss engineer George de Mestral, seeing how well prickly burrs stuck to his clothing and his dog, came up with the idea of Velcro.

You can learn a lot by observing nature. If you've ever watched Canada geese, you've probably heard a lot of honking and noticed the V formation they use in flight. Both of these traits are part of their group dynamics. Try a few of their strategies with your friends or youth group to help you work well together.

Honking

Geese honk to encourage one another. That keeps them soaring high in the sky.

Encourage others in your group:

- Tell members you appreciate them.
- Thank members when they work and when they complete a task.
- Praise members who try hard.
- Praise the team for success.

When threatened or excited, geese make loud, rapid honks to get the attention of the flock. When they prepare for takeoff, they create a noisy chorus. You can use and pay attention to noise in your group:

- Celebrate with a noisy cheer at the beginning and ending of an activity to build team spirit.
- Listen up if someone shouts for help.
- Remember that male and female geese make different sounds. Let the guys and girls in your group express themselves and their perspectives.

V Formation

Flying in V formation creates downdrafts that help the birds in the back fly faster and with less effort. There's also an upwash to help those ahead fly easier. When the bird at the front of the V tires, another takes over. Sharing the load helps everyone fly farther and faster.

Follow their lead:

- Rotate leadership so everyone gains the experience of being a leader.
- Watch the leader. If he or she seems overwhelmed, sick, or is facing challenges at home or school, suggest a temporary leader to fill in.
- Consider using different leaders for different projects. That way the group can benefit from everyone's strengths.
- Partner weaker members with stronger ones. Let experienced members teach new ones in their areas of strength.
- Pause and notice how members are doing. Let the ones accomplishing a lot be an inspiration to the group.

By flying in a V shape, geese can see one another better. That helps them notice if a member gets tired and needs encouragement. Do the same:

- Use a circle to pray so you can see one another.
- Look at one another and notice body language and facial expressions.
- Encourage the quieter members to share thoughts and ideas.

Scouting

Sometimes a smaller group of geese will break apart from the main group. These geese are a scouting party, looking for a better draft and more favorable flying conditions.

Getting more information for your group is good:

- Have several members check out opportunities for the group. They might find out about concerts, community service projects, hurting members in the church, or fun activities where you can team up with another youth group. Let them report back with suggestions and ideas.

Loyalty

Geese mate for life. When one member falls back from illness or gets hurt, two fly with it. The other two remain until the weak one recovers or dies. That's loyalty!

Be loyal to the members of your group:

- Support one another by listening.
- Stay with someone in need and bring along a helper.
- Never give up on a teammate. If a member of your group misses getting together, follow up with a card, encouraging text, or a comment on social media.

- Be supportive. Be generous. Be there. Smiles make everyone feel welcome. Never gossip or put down other members.
- Pray as a group.

Clustering

Canada geese group into family clusters when they land.

Keep your group strong:

- Encourage members in their relationships with their families.
- Get to know the parents and siblings of teammates. That helps their families be supportive of your group.

Groups of guys and girls don't always naturally get along. God's Spirit helps bind us together with common values and beliefs. And by looking at nature—especially geese—we can be birds of a feather who naturally flock together.

WORD OF TRUTH

Make every effort to keep yourselves united in the Spirit, binding yourselves together with peace.
EPHESIANS 4:3

Verbal First-Aid Kit

Words can wound deeply, stabbing us in the heart. But words can also bring healing.

Words are both our greatest weapons and our most effective "bandages." Inspiring words lift a person's spirit. Kind words bring encouragement. Loving words help stitch up torn hearts and soothe hurt feelings.

Doctors train for years and endure difficult schooling to learn how to heal physical wounds. Using our words to help heal emotional wounds also takes practice and careful thought.

What words would you put in your "medicine bag"? Write down what you might say to help in these situations.

Stethoscope—to check the heart condition.

_____

Blood pressure cuff—to help someone calm down.

_____

Bandage—to cover a wound when someone's been cut down.

_____

Ointment—to soothe pain.

_____

Stitches—to bind deep wounds.

_____

Ice pack—to cool off a heated situation.

_____

As much as we can try to help our friends, there's no substitute for the Great Physician. Jesus came to heal the sick and brokenhearted. His ministry on earth was filled with miraculous healings. But God not only wants to cure our physical ailments, he also longs to mend our hearts.

When you talk with a hurting friend, try to do the same.

WORD OF TRUTH

[God] heals the brokenhearted and bandages their wounds.

PSALM 147:3

Manly Words

Alex and Mason spent as much time as they could in the mountains. Camping, hiking, backpacking—any activity was on the table . . . except rock climbing. While Mason was part mountain goat, Alex felt as wobbly as a newborn giraffe when he walked up a rock.

During their senior year, the two friends took off for a trip to the mountains. Strapping on backpacks, they started up an isolated trail. Suddenly, the path ended at a rock face.

"We can totally climb this," Mason said. "Just follow me and use the same handholds that I use."

Alex had a decision to make: hike around or climb up. Testosterone trumped intelligence, and Alex agreed to climb. For the first seventy feet, things went fine. But then it happened. Alex missed a handhold and found himself slipping down the rock. His fingers clawed into the granite to no avail. He slid faster and faster.

"Grab something," Mason shouted as his friend looked up at him in terror.

Alex tried. But he kept gaining speed as he headed for a fifteen-foot drop. At the last moment, he lunged to his right and caught a large handhold. His body jerked to a stop, just a few feet from doom.

Knees bloody, hands like hamburger, Alex managed to climb down the mountain with Mason's help. Driving home, Alex realized his near-death experience had forever changed one of the strongest muscles in his body: his tongue.

Realizing that any words could be his last, Alex started to

watch everything that came out of his mouth. Instead of putting down his sister, he started telling her that he loved her. He talked more openly with his parents. Alex changed from the sarcastic, silent type into a guy who told his friends and family how much he cared for them.

First Corinthians 13:1 says without love words become "a noisy gong or a clanging cymbal." Sometimes guys can think saying, "I love you" sounds girly. Don't wait for a near-death experience to change your mind. When we show and tell our family and friends that we love them, it's the manliest words that can be spoken.

WORD OF TRUTH

If I could speak all the languages of earth and of angels, but didn't love others, I would only be a noisy gong or a clanging cymbal.

1 CORINTHIANS 13:1

PART THREE

Up to Date

Are you up to dating? That's a question your parents will probably help you answer. Many families have different opinions on the proper time to start dating (and sometimes that opinion is "never").

Teen romances can be hot, but they often flame out. Just ask Romeo and Juliet. Oh wait, we can't. But we can learn something from that cautionary tale—date with discretion.

This last section of the book will help you avoid some of the pitfalls and problems with dating. You'll also pick up on some of the differences that drive guys and girls into relationships . . . or out of them.

From breakups to arguments to sex, dating brings plenty of pressure. So really, are you up for it? Are you ready to get better equipped to handle a girl-guy relationship?

Love—
It's All Greek to Me!

for Guys & Girls

I love chocolate! I love football! I love purple! I love you!

The word *love* gets thrown around . . . a lot. English is one of the most complex and diverse languages in the world, but it's pretty limited when it comes to the word *love*. It can be used to describe many things.

But what *exactly* does L-O-V-E mean?

Love is used both casually and intimately. You can say it to express

- desire for sweets or objects,
- enthusiasm for sports or other activities,
- care for people,
- affection for close friends and family,
- worship for God,
- closeness within marriage, and
- a variety of other things.

In the Bible, God is described as love (see 1 John 4:8). God shows his love for us in many ways. He expresses his love in the beauty of creation. He demonstrated his love by sending his Son to earth. Jesus displayed ultimate love by dying for our sins so we could be forgiven and know God personally.

This kind of love is *waaaaay* more powerful than the sentiment we express when we say, "I love chocolate ice cream."

We use a single word—*love*—to describe many feelings. But it was different in biblical times. Love was more deeply embedded in the culture, so different words were used to describe different kinds of love.

To make this more clear (and frosty), take a trip to Canada's Nunavik region. The Inuit people live in a culture of snow and ice. They have fifty different words to describe different types of snow. A wet snow is called *matsaaruti*, while a powdery snow is referred to as *pukak*. It's easy for sled dogs to travel through *matsaaruti*, while *pukak* can be a pain. Knowing the specific *kind* of snow is important to the Inuits.

That's the way it was in biblical times. People wanted to know *exactly* what kind of love was being talked about. The Bible uses four Greek words for love, each with a different meaning.

Phileo (fil-ay-oh)

This refers to the brotherly love of friendship. Ever wonder why Philadelphia is called the "City of Brotherly Love"? Blame the Greeks. *Phileo* love describes the feelings you have for teammates, close friends, and certain objects.

Storge (stor-gay)

This word describes the love shared by family members. If you want to make your mom's day, walk up to her and say, "I *storge* you." This kind of love is built on loyalty, family bonds, and affection.

Agape (ah-gah-pay)

This is the love that Christ calls us to. It seeks the best for others, while expecting nothing in return. *Agape* love is unconditional. It's the way God loves us. It's love in a spiritual sense. To give *agape*, it's best to be tapped into its source—God. This is a committed love that lasts in good times and bad. *Agape* can be used for the way a husband loves a wife or the way God loves his church.

Eros (eh-ross)

Our culture is infatuated with *eros*, which makes sense, because *eros* is used to describe feelings of lust and infatuation. The word refers to physical love, sexual desire, and longing. The English word *erotic* finds its roots in this love. When we look at someone and feel attracted physically, that's *eros*. *Eros* can be misused, but it can also be beautiful and bonding. The special expression of *eros* love should be saved for marriage.

Love is one of the most powerful forces on the planet. When we understand it, we'll be more prepared to express love in the way God intended. Our heavenly Father doesn't embrace cheap love. He wants us to love deeply—just like he loves us.

How can you better appreciate love?

☐ Discover real love by understanding God's love for you.
☐ Observe how committed Christians help others.
☐ Watch how the members of a happily married couple put each other first.
☐ Read the Bible and look for the different ways the word *love* is used.
☐ Notice how a parent cares for his or her child.

WORD OF TRUTH

We love each other because he loved us first.
1 JOHN 4:19

Girl talk — Words to Save

"I love you." Those three words change a relationship. They declare deep feelings. Those three words are also overused, often misused, and can be wielded as a weapon.

A guy might say that phrase as a signal that he's ready to get more physical. He may use "I love you" to pressure you to go further physically than you want to. For a girl, the phrase might mean a deeper emotional commitment and desire for a long-term relationship.

No matter how the L-word is used, it changes things.

Because dropping an L-bomb is so powerful, don't do it recklessly. Wait and save those words for when you really mean it—when you are old enough for marriage and a lasting relationship.

The Bible says there are three great forces in the world: faith, hope, and love. But the greatest is love (see 1 Corinthians 13:13). Tossing around love only gets us in trouble.

We may *love* pepperoni pizza and cute puppies, but when we tell a guy we love him, it hits him at his core. With the love of the right girl, a guy can feel like he's Superman.

In the Old Testament, Jacob loved Rachel, but her dad tricked Jacob into marrying his other daughter, Leah. Jacob then worked seven more years to win Rachel as his bride. The time seemed short and the work seemed easy, because he loved her (see Genesis 29:20). Love waits, knowing the reward will be worth it.

So be sure to think long and hard before you speak the L-word. In your dating relationships, you can use different phrases to show you care:

- "You're amazing."
- "You crushed it."
- "You're a man-imal."

Okay, the last one is terrible, but you'll think of something. Because waiting to say "I love you" is worth it.

WORD OF TRUTH

Jacob served seven years for Rachel, and they seemed to him but a few days because of the love he had for her.
GENESIS 29:20, ESV

Guy talk

The Power of Love

You can't watch a teen flick without seeing two characters tenderly holding each other and saying, "I love you." The fault is *not* in their stars—it's with us for watching the movie in the first place. Real life often dishes out the same menu of words. We walk down the school hallway and see guys and girls holding hands and saying, "I love you" as they leave each other to go to class.

Love is one of the most overused words in the English language. Most of the time overused words lose their meaning. They become just background noise.

But *love* is different. It *never* loses its power.

Don't believe it? Try this. After hanging out with a group of girls, walk up to one that you really like and say, "I love you." No, wait. That's too dangerous. Go drop an L-bomb on your mom. What happens?

God designed girls so that their greatest desire is to be loved. When they hear that word, it's like water for somebody dying of thirst. It feeds and builds them up. Because of that, don't dish out the L-word until you're ready for a serious commitment, which may mean a relationship heading toward marriage.

Our friends may look at love as just a fuzzy feeling or as a nice thing to say to somebody. But in Romans, the apostle Paul tells us not to copy the world. We need to let God transform the way we think about everything, including love.

We've got to look at love the way God sees it. In God's eyes, love means sacrifice. That's not very sexy, but it's the truth. The most famous verse in the Bible says, "This is how God loved the world: He gave his one and only Son, so that everyone who believes in him will not perish but have eternal life" (John 3:16).

Until you're ready to sacrifice your time, your individuality, and even your life for a girl, it's best to wait to tell her that you love her.

WORD OF TRUTH

Don't copy the behavior and customs of this world, but let God transform you into a new person by changing the way you think.

ROMANS 12:2

Warning Signs

When you see a wet-paint sign, do you reach out and touch the wall? When you hear a fire alarm, do you ignore it until you see smoke?

Hopefully, you answered both of those questions with a resounding *no*. It's always best to trust warning signs and avoid danger.

When it comes to guys, it'd be nice if they came with warning signs. Some do. Well, sort of. If a guy's wearing a shirt that says, "I'm not lazy. I'm marinating!" it's probably smart to run away. Other signs are more subtle. If you miss these signs, you may end up hanging out with guys who could hurt you or cause you to make poor choices. So beware and watch for these red flags:

- Control issues can show up as anger, overpowering your opinions, and disrespect for rules. This guy could become abusive in a relationship.
- Real compliments are nice and show interest, but excessive or false flattery can be a warning. A guy may use flattery to get what he wants, and that's often sex.
- Does he act differently around his friends or parents than he does around you? You want a guy whose actions and words are consistent.
- Does he always brag about himself or show off? This can reveal insecurity and self-centeredness. He's probably too wrapped up in himself to care about your feelings.

- He walks up and wraps his arms around you—even if he doesn't know you very well. That can show possessiveness and a desire to get intimate fast.
- How does a guy drive? Does he follow the speed limit? If he goes too fast or ignores stop signs, he may be dangerous . . . to your safety and to pushing your boundaries.

Watching a guy that you're interested in for warning signs is wise. See what signals he's sending out. The Bible isn't kidding when it says, "Bad company ruins good morals" (1 Corinthians 15:33, ESV). If we get involved with a "bad" boy, we'll probably be pulled down . . . even if we try to lift him up.

By being aware of warning signs and paying attention to them, we'll know which guys are truly deserving of our attention.

WORD OF TRUTH

Do not be deceived: "Bad company ruins good morals."
1 CORINTHIANS 15:33, ESV

Mighty Samson's Mighty Problem

Have you ever read Samson's story in the Bible? The guy was an absolute stud! God wanted Samson to live a strict life according to God's laws, and he gave Samson amazing strength. Samson's feats are legendary:

- He killed a lion with his bare hands (see Judges 14:5-6).
- He killed one thousand men with the jawbone of a donkey (see Judges 15:15). (Talk about sinking your teeth into a fight!)
- He tore off a city gate and carried it to the top of a mountain (see Judges 16:3).

As amazing as Samson's strength was, his weakness was similarly amazing. Samson seemed to have one thing on his mind when he looked at a woman. It's the same thing that most guys have on their minds. Samson's eyes ruled his decision-making. And his eyes often led him to the wrong woman.

How bad was it?

Well, Samson chose a wife by spotting a woman in the distance, going home, and telling his father, "Get her for me! She looks good to me" (Judges 14:3).

No conversation.

No getting to know the young woman.

Just, "She looks good, so I want to marry her."

Guess what? The marriage ended in disaster.

But Samson didn't learn. His relationship with a woman named Delilah started out bad and only got worse from there (you can read about it in Judges 16).

So what's the lesson?

Make relationship decisions about girls with your brain, not with your eyes.

Our eyes will get us into trouble when it comes to girls. God created girls to be attractive to us, so it's natural to be drawn to them. But be careful about where you focus your eyes and what you're basing your attraction on. Lasting beauty is an inner character trait—not something we can see.

Pray to God to help you be wise, to be attracted to the right kind of girls, and to stay pure in your relationships. If you do that, you'll have far more relational strength than Samson ever had.

WORD OF TRUTH

Samson told his father, "Get her for me! She looks good to me."

JUDGES 14:3

First Dates

First dates can be exciting . . . and awkward.

Where do we go?
What do we talk about?
Who pays?
Should we go with a group or alone as a couple?

We can learn a lot of dating dos and don'ts by looking at famous couples in the Bible. Boaz and Ruth are Jesus Christ's great-great-great (and a ton more greats) grandparents. Ruth had just moved to a new country to help her mother-in-law. Boaz was a powerful landowner.

Check out how their first date went down . . . well, sort of.

Boaz: Hey, see that cute girl? Where'd she come from?

Ralph: She just moved to town. Her mother-in-law sent her to visit our church community service project. She's been here all day, and wow! She's smart and works hard.

Boaz: Hmm, a gal with brains and who isn't afraid to get a little dirty helping others. It's time we met.

[Boaz strolls over to Ruth and waits for a pause in her conversation.]

Boaz: I haven't seen you before. I'm Boaz. It's good to meet you.

Ruth: Thanks. I've heard of you. You're pretty popular.

Boaz: Well, I've been here awhile and helped lead a lot of service projects.

Ruth: I moved here last week. It's been a tough year for my family. We're just trying to trust God.

Boaz: That's cool. I want to grow closer to God too. Maybe we can study about him together.

Ruth: Thanks for inviting me. I appreciate that.

Boaz: It's time for a break. Do you want to grab something to eat?

Ruth: Sure.

Boaz: Sit here, and I'll get our snacks.

Ruth: Wow! Smart and manners too! I like that.

[Boaz serves Ruth and introduces her to his friends.]

Did you learn anything from that scene?
Girls, look at these things:

- Guys are drawn to girls who are smart and have dreams.
- When a guy invites you on a date, remember to express appreciation.
- Be aware of a guy's reputation. You can learn a lot.
- It's best to get to know one another in a safe, public place.

Guys, take note:

- There's a lot more to a girl than her physical appearance.
- Character counts. Look for girls who are smart and kind and love God.
- Take the lead in meeting a girl. Be yourself, and don't try to use pickup lines.

If you begin liking a guy/girl, talk with your parents. They'll probably want to set some rules for getting to know the opposite sex. If your parents allow you to date, expect them to create guidelines for how old you need to be to go out and if you can hang out only in groups. Be ready to tell a potential date about your standards before you go out.

As you plan for a first date, give careful consideration to where to go. You may want to start with a public place where you feel comfortable. Sometimes it's best, especially if you're younger, to be part of a group when you spend time with the opposite sex.

Don't forget to focus on friendship instead of physical attraction. The best long-term relationships start as friendships. That's what Boaz and Ruth did.

WORD OF TRUTH

At mealtime Boaz called to her, "Come over here, and help yourself to some food. You can dip your bread in the sour wine." So she sat with his harvesters, and Boaz gave her some roasted grain to eat. She ate all she wanted and still had some left over.

RUTH 2:14

Girl Talk

Waiting for Mr. Right

All your friends have boyfriends (at least it seems that way). You deserve to be treated like a princess too. What girl doesn't want to be cherished? But you probably won't find the right guy for years. Some girls get tired of waiting and settle for Prince Mediocre when they deserve Prince Charming. Be patient. Act like a lady, and expect to be treated like one.

There's more to waiting than just sitting around. You can use that time to develop godly character traits that will make you the kind of woman Mr. Right would want to marry. A relationship works best when it's between two healthy people with similar values and beliefs. But as you work on yourself, you can also decide what you want in a husband. After all, if you don't know what you want, you won't recognize it when you see it.

Start by looking around at the men in your life. Who do you respect the most? How do they treat women? How do they talk with their friends? Watch happily married couples and note the good qualities in those men.

You can also learn a lot from God's Word. Sometimes the message is obvious. Other times you'll have to dig a little. Read 1 Corinthians 13:4-7 (it's printed on the next page). Pick out some of the characteristics you'd like to see in your future spouse.

Then add some of your own ideas. Don't cheat yourself. Be honest and thoughtful.

Top Ten Qualities You Want in a Husband

10. _____

9. _____

8. _____

7. _____

6. _____

5. _____

4. _____

3. _____

2. _____

1. _____

As you meet guys, see how they measure up. Don't be afraid to be choosy. If a guy doesn't fit your high expectations, he's probably not the guy for you right now. Don't rush God's timing when it comes to relationships. And remember, not every girl will meet Mr. Right and get married. God knows some of us will serve him better if we're single.

Share your desires with God. Pray for your potential future husband. To lock in your standards, memorize the verse about true love. Then you'll always be able to remember that you're waiting for Mr. Right . . . not Mr. Right Now.

 WORD OF TRUTH

Love is patient and kind; love does not envy or boast; it is not arrogant or rude. It does not insist on its own way; it is not irritable or resentful; it does not rejoice at wrongdoing, but rejoices with the truth. Love bears all things, believes all things, hopes all things, endures all things.
1 CORINTHIANS 13:4-7, ESV

It's a Date!

Courtship versus dating. Group dates versus one-on-one. If you're a Christian guy who wants to get to know a girl, it's not easy. Many families have differing views of dating. If your family (or the family of the girl you're interested in) believes in waiting to date, follow the rules. It could save you a lot of embarrassment and heartache.

Asking a girl to go out with you isn't easy. Just thinking about inviting a girl on a date is enough to cause some guys to sweat profusely and drop forty IQ points. Check this out:

"Hey, Kylie, would you . . . you know, maybe want to . . . Uh, how about you and me going to, you know, see that new movie this Friday?"

Does that sound familiar?

Instead of one-on-one dates, a lot of guys prefer the non-date, or group date, for many reasons.

1. It's easier to ask a girl to go. Look at this: "Hey, Kylie, a bunch of us are going to the new movie this Friday. Do you want to come?" If she says no, it's no big deal. It wasn't a date anyway, so your self-esteem doesn't suffer. She's rejecting the activity, not you.
2. Group dates are less stressful. You don't have to come up with a ton of clever conversation starters. When you're with a group, there are a ton of conversations you can join or just listen to.
3. A girl can read too much into a one-on-one date. You may just want to be friends and get to know her better,

but she may think you want an exclusive, long-term relationship.

4. It's safer. When it's just the two of you alone in a car or movie theater, it's possible to be tempted to get physical. Having other friends along can keep you accountable. In John's Gospel, Jesus says that he's the vine and we're the branches (see 15:5). Notice that Jesus didn't say we're the *branch*. God wants us to grow stronger with him and around other believers.

When it comes to building relationships with girls, it's always better to stay close to God and our Christian friends.

WORD OF TRUTH

I am the vine; you are the branches. Those who remain in me, and I in them, will produce much fruit.
JOHN 15:5

Breaking Up Is Hard to Do

Dating can be great. If your family allows you to date, you may experience all kinds of excitement getting to know a guy. But as great as it can be, most dating relationships end with a breakup. And that can be really hard.

Google "break-up stories" and you'll read horror stories of couples breaking up over a text, through a friend, or with hot soup being thrown. Actually, don't google "break-up stories," just know it's not easy to break up. It's even harder to do it the *right* way.

When you realize a relationship isn't healthy, isn't what you want, or doesn't have a future, you need to get out. So what do you do?

Be Real

Speak to your boyfriend in person. That shows respect and kindness. Texting a guy that you're breaking up with him doesn't honor the relationship.

Be Kind

Remind the guy he has great qualities and that you enjoyed getting to know him. The good times were good, but you know it's best for the two of you to go separate ways.

Be Clear

Let him know you are not ready to continue the relationship. Say, "I don't want to be your girlfriend anymore." Give constructive reasons for your decision, but be nice about it. For example, "We argue too much and can't seem to find common interests. I don't think we are good together."

Be Compassionate

Let him know you understand this might hurt, and you'll be praying for him. Share that in the future you hope both of you will be able to see that it was for the best.

Be Firm

Remind him that you've decided that breaking up is the best decision for you. If you don't want to be friends going forward, let him know by saying something like, "It'd be best if we didn't talk to each other for a while." Don't lead him on or give him hope of getting back together if you don't see that happening.

Be Smart

Break up in a public place or with some of your friends or family close by. Some breakups can turn ugly, especially if you said that you loved the guy or went too far physically. Pick the setting. Let your friends and family know what you plan to do and ask them to pray for you.

Sometimes breakups turn into arguments. If you're able, try not to allow that to happen. The Bible says that by being gentle and humble, we can avoid quarreling. A breakup without quarreling: now that's the right way to do it.

WORD OF TRUTH

They must not slander anyone and must avoid quarreling. Instead, they should be gentle and show true humility to everyone.
TITUS 3:2

Guy talk

The Big Breakup

Derrick knew the relationship wasn't working. Rachel was smothering him.

Before school: she was there.

At lunch: she was there.

After school: she was there.

At church: she was there.

Over the weekend: she was there.

On his phone: she was *always* there. Nearly every text and call Derrick got came from her . . . even in the middle of the night.

Derrick liked Rachel. But he had other interests, like hanging out with his friends, playing video games, and trying to get good grades. Now Derrick's schoolwork and friendships were suffering. Enough was enough.

"Send her a text," Devon said. "It's quick and painless."

"No, just ignore her," Tyler said. "She'll get the message eventually."

"This is the way to do it," Zach jumped in. "Sit her down and say, 'It's not you. It's me.' I saw that work on a TV show."

Derrick was smart enough to know it was time to break up. He also was smart enough to recognize really bad advice. Instead of listening to his friends, Derrick listened to God. He knew he should break things off with Rachel in the same way he'd like to be treated if a girl broke up with him.

The next day he took Rachel aside after school. He sat down with her face-to-face and explained his feelings.

"I'm not ready to be in such a serious relationship," he said.

"I do care about you, but I also know the healthiest decision for me right now. My grades are slipping, which is all my fault, because I'm spending so much time with you. I don't expect you to understand my decision to break up, but it's the best one for me right now."

Derrick was honest while also being kind. He knew his words would hurt Rachel. But he also knew she'd be able to deal with her feelings and move forward more easily if he handled the breakup well.

Treat others the way you want to be treated. That's what Jesus taught, and it's always a great way to go.

WORD OF TRUTH

Do to others whatever you would like them to do to you. This is the essence of all that is taught in the law and the prophets.
MATTHEW 7:12

Different Is Good

God made guys and girls different. Sure, we look different. But did you know our very cells are different? Our organs are different too. Gals have smaller lungs, but larger stomachs, kidneys, and livers than guys do. Guys and girls aren't even wired the same way. Our brains are different anatomically, chemically, hormonally, and physiologically. Just look at this:

Guy's Brain	Girl's Brain
Higher ability to systematize	Lower ability to compartmentalize (all flows together)
Lower ability to multitask	Higher ability to multitask
Higher ability to control emotions	Lower ability to control emotions
Lower relational orientation and more physically oriented	Higher relational orientation and highly empathetic
Stress response—act first, think later	Stress response—think and feel before acting

Our brain differences mean we respond and act differently. But those responses can complement each other.

Do you remember what God said after he created the first man? He noted, "It is not good for the man to be alone. I will make a helper who is just right for him" (Genesis 2:18). God knew Adam needed someone else in his life. He needed a woman. Men and women need one another. They have different perspectives and abilities that balance each other out. Check out some of these other differences:

It's in the Male

- ☐ Say few words
- ☐ Like adventure
- ☐ Stick to one topic at a time
- ☐ Sometimes think about nothing—a guy's mind can be blank
- ☐ Are very visual!
- ☐ Physical attraction is a big driver in relationships
- ☐ Live in the moment
- ☐ Don't think about other things when focused on a task
- ☐ Punch, poke, and get physical in greeting friends
- ☐ Seldom take a hint
- ☐ Don't dwell on words and focus more on actions

It's a Girl Thing

- ☐ Talk more
- ☐ Active minds are constantly thinking
- ☐ Are more emotional
- ☐ Switch conversations and thoughts rapidly and easily
- ☐ Look for subtext and deeper meanings behind words
- ☐ Have more complex hormonal patterns
- ☐ Use hints to get what they want

Some of the differences between guys and girls can seem silly, especially when it comes to hairy, grunting guys. But understanding and accepting these differences can help us see from the other person's perspective when we interact with each other. Our differences can make communicating more difficult, but they also bring excitement and adventure into a relationship. Remember, too, that we are each unique and some of the attributes listed above are generalizations and may not apply to you. You might be a girl who talks less but loves adventure. That's okay.

God knew what he was doing when he made men and women. By embracing our differences and seeing how they complement each other and reflect our Creator, we can have better and healthier relationships.

WORD OF TRUTH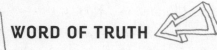

The Lord God said, "It is not good for the man to be alone. I will make a helper who is just right for him."
GENESIS 2:18

Lies Girls Believe

How would you feel if, on your birthday, someone handed you a gift that someone else already opened—a present that was unwrapped, used, and passed around to other people?

You have a gift that's worth saving. You can see where this is going, right? It's your purity. When you have sex with a guy, you give away the most intimate part of yourself. Sex connects a guy and girl in body and spirit. It's a deep expression of commitment.

If you think you're not pure because of your past, remember that God forgives you. You can give yourself a new start on purity by beginning to follow God's will in this area.

Sex is a gift that should be saved for marriage, but the world we live in says something different. You might hear that sex is no big deal. It's just casual fun or something people do to show they like each other. Those are lies. There are plenty of others . . .

Lie: Sex is safe.

There's no such thing as safe sex, except within a marriage relationship between a husband and wife who are faithful to each other. Sexually transmitted diseases continue to grow. Some STDs are incurable. Others cause infertility.

Lie: Sex will bring you closer.

A study of 100,000 women linked sex before marriage with unhappiness in marriage and sexual intimacy. Many couples break up, even after having sex.

Lie: Teens can't control their urges.

That's ridiculous. You're more than a walking storm of hormones. As daughters of our heavenly Father, we're specially equipped to make good decisions. Self-control is a fruit of the Spirit. Only go out with guys who display a similar "fruit." With God helping us, there's no temptation that we can't overcome (see 1 Corinthians 10:13).

Lie: It's okay if you're in love.

If a guy truly loves you, he will want the best for you. He'll protect you—and that includes your purity. Waiting shows respect. Pushing someone too far sexually reveals selfishness.

The Truth

God is smarter than us. He designed sex for marriage. He knows sex is an expression of love within marriage and for the purpose of bringing new life into this world. Seek to share God's view: sex is a precious gift.

WORD OF TRUTH

Let marriage be held in honor among all, and let the marriage bed be undefiled, for God will judge the sexually immoral and adulterous.
HEBREWS 13:4, ESV

True Love Waits

Girls want to be loved. Actually, love is something everybody needs, but it's especially important to girls. Some guys will tell a girl they love her just to persuade her to have sex with them.

Sex isn't something you should convince a girl to do. It's not a game, just like a girl isn't a conquest. Despite popular opinion, there's no such thing as a meaningless hookup.

Sex is a gift that God designed to be shared by a man and woman in marriage. If you're not ready to be married and become a father, you shouldn't be thinking about having sex.

But *not* thinking about sex is nearly impossible. Researchers say guys think about sex a few times every hour. Controlling your mind is the key to keeping your sexual desires in check.

God created guys to be attracted to women. He told us to be fruitful and multiply. But God also gave us his Spirit, which helps us to have self-control. When it comes to sex, the best way we can thank God for his gift is to show self-control.

Controlling yourself can be hard if you really like (or even love) a girl. You have to set boundaries and be smart about not being alone together. That's because true love waits . . . for a lot of reasons.

- Waiting shows respect. Using a girl to fulfill your sexual desires is not respecting her. Show respect to a girl by protecting her purity.
- Waiting shows selflessness. Pushing a girl to go too far sexually is selfish. The Bible tells us love is not self-seeking (see 1 Corinthians 13:5).

- Waiting shows protection. Girls want to feel protected and cared for by a guy. If you're in a relationship with a girl, you need to guard all areas of her life, including her sexuality.

God knows sex can be a powerful temptation. That's why the Bible says to run from sexual sin (see 1 Corinthians 6:18). Honor God and honor your future wife with how you handle your sexual desires. Waiting is hard . . . but it's also worth it.

WORD OF TRUTH

Let there be no sexual immorality, impurity, or greed among you. Such sins have no place among God's people.
EPHESIANS 5:3

Girl talk   Crushed by Your Crush!

You just got rejected by a guy. Dumped, dismissed, tossed in the trash heap. Well, maybe not literally, but that's how it feels. Or maybe you saw your latest crush with another girl. And it hurts!

Instead of running up to the guy and screaming, "Well, this is what you'll be missin'," take a little time to heal. It's okay to hold a private pity party.

1. Invite only one guest: Jesus. He was rejected by a close friend and understands the pain. Jesus was chosen and is precious to God . . . and so are you.

2. Pamper yourself by taking a relaxing bath, eating a special treat, or listening to your favorite Christian music.

3. Light a candle. Read Psalm 6 or Psalm 13. Other people in the Bible held pity parties, including King David. Remember that God has plans for you and that he listens to you. As the candle melts away, your hurt will too.

4. List your hurts, problems, and worries. Circle the one that causes you the most pain. Pray over the rejection list and give it to God. Save the circled one for last. Ask forgiveness, if needed. Rip up the paper and throw it in the trash.

5. Write positive things about yourself, regarding your appearance, personality, interests, talents, and things only God sees. Circle ones that lift your spirits. Praise God for each of these and keep this paper. Put it where you can read it over and over again.

6. Have a love feast. Take some bread and water or grape juice and enjoy breaking bread in God's presence. It's called an *agape* meal. God loves you! Read John 6:35, 53-58. Jesus is the Bread of Life and the Living Water. You can count on his strength.

7. After your healing party, don't be afraid to face your crush. Smile and wish him the best.

Crushes will come and go. Jesus will be with you always—and you're precious to him!

WORD OF TRUTH

You come to him, a living stone rejected by men but in the sight of God chosen and precious.

1 PETER 2:4, ESV

Guy talk — In the Dumps

You just got dumped by a girl. If you're like most guys, two thoughts immediately come to mind:

- I have to get her back!
- I need to get an even better girlfriend to make her jealous.

Actually, many thoughts may pop into your head, including, *I'm so bummed. She was great. What's wrong with me? Nobody's ever going to love me.*

As guys, we often try to push down our emotions. Feelings are hard to deal with, especially feelings that come with getting dumped. When a girl tells you that she doesn't like you anymore, it hurts. A lot!

Feeling pain is normal after a breakup. But God often uses pain in our lives to teach us something important. Do you remember the first time you touched a hot stove? It hurt, right? And you probably never did it again, because you realized what would happen.

Instead of wallowing in your pain or pushing it aside, see if there's anything you can learn from it. Were you too controlling in the relationship? Did you show the girl the respect and care she desired? Were you selfish? Were you smothering?

You might not have the answers to those questions right away, but some introspection after a breakup can be a good thing.

And as far as those first two thoughts are concerned, don't go there. Trying to get a girl back can make you seem needy and desperate. Just like a greased pig, if you try to hold on too tightly, a girl will slip away. Going after a "better" girl just shows you didn't learn anything from the breakup. In any relationship, both people make it work or cause it to fail. You have to own your part and look for areas where you can grow.

Even though it doesn't feel good, option three is the place to be. Let yourself hurt. Work through your emotions. And always remember you can go to God and receive his healing mercy. God is always faithful.

WORD OF TRUTH

The faithful love of the LORD never ends! His mercies never cease. Great is his faithfulness; his mercies begin afresh each morning.
LAMENTATIONS 3:22-23

Ex Marks the Spot

for Guys & Girls

Most relationships end with a breakup. It's sad, but true. And when your ex goes to the same school or church, you can end up running into him or her . . . a lot. Those close encounters can often be awkward, especially if the relationship ended badly or if one person wishes the relationship was still going.

Take this quiz to see how you'd react in these ex-sighting situations.

1. You break up with a guy/girl. The next time you see him/her you
   a. smile, look him/her in the eye, and say, "How are you doing?"
   b. turn the other way and try to hide.
   c. turn to your friend and start talking about your ex.
   d. cringe, swallow, and walk past without looking at your ex.

2. A friend asks why you broke up. You
   a. start sobbing.
   b. tell the truth in a kind way.
   c. dish on your ex, and put him or her down for the way you were treated.
   d. quickly change the subject.

3. You're in youth group with your ex. The leader asks the two of you to do something together. You
   a. rush out of the room in an emotional huff.
   b. smile and do your best to be nice and work together.

c. shout, "How could you ask me to do that after I was stabbed in the heart?"

d. agree, but barely speak to your ex during the process.

4. You still have his jacket (or her sweater). You
   a. spill stuff on it, crumple it up, and then return it.
   b. cry all over it and sleep with it.
   c. wash and return it.
   d. toss it in the back of your closet.

5. You have photos of your ex on your phone. You
   a. print one as a target and throw darts at it.
   b. leave them.
   c. delete them all.
   d. create a mean meme and post it on the Internet.

6. You find out your ex is dating one of your friends. You
   a. stop talking to that friend.
   b. pray that they will be a good match for one another.
   c. tell your friend about your ex's faults.
   d. talk about both of them behind their backs.

After a breakup, you might be tempted to do the hurtful things. You may feel so down that you eat only ice cream and wear only sweats for a month. Maybe you sob and let your emotions show. Or you might smile and be kind when you see the other person again.

(Note: This last option takes a lot of maturity and usually lots of time.)

Go back and look at your answers to the quiz. The hurtful choices (1c, 2c, 3c, 4a, 5d, 6d, etc.) may seem funny. But taking

revenge and spreading rumors usually hurts you more than your intended target.

The more mature options (1a, 2b, 3b, 4c, 5b, 6b, etc.) are the ones to aim at. Forgiveness is key after a breakup. You'll know you've forgiven your ex when you can pray for and still want the best for the person. It doesn't happen all at once. At first you may want your ex's face to explode in one giant zit. Ask for God to help you respond with grace and maturity.

In the Bible, Jesus promised his followers a gift—a peace that the world can't understand. Whenever you face a difficult time like a breakup, remember God's gift. Ask him to bring peace to your heart and mind.

The emotional responses of tears, anger, and sadness are natural after a breakup. Let yourself heal and don't be afraid to feel sad. But pull yourself together with prayer and the help of friends. Because if you decide to date, you probably will run into your exes . . . unless they all live in Texas (which works for a song, not real life).

WORD OF TRUTH

I am leaving you with a gift—peace of mind and heart. And the peace I give is a gift the world cannot give. So don't be troubled or afraid.

JOHN 14:27

Girl talk

Fast-Acting Friendship

Relationships aren't static; they constantly change. When we ignore a relationship, it gets worse. But if we put time and energy into a relationship, it can grow and develop. Part of being a loyal, honest, and good friend is being active in the friendship.

Commitment in a guy-girl relationship is different. A forever relationship with a guy, like marriage, is probably years away for you. You're still growing emotionally, physically, mentally, and spiritually. What you look for in a guy will change over the years, until you find a guy who loves you, loves God, and supports you in living out God's will for your life.

But you're not too young to enjoy a close, wholesome friendship with a guy. Your parents probably have rules about any dating relationship. Follow those. Although it may not seem like it, your parents have been in your situation and dealt with the same feelings you have. They make rules to protect you from heartache.

Group activities are a great way to build a connection. And if you decide to go deeper with a certain guy, you can discuss what your friendship means to him. But before that conversation happens, it's a good idea to discuss these points:

- We'll talk ____ times a week.
- We'll get together ____ times a week. In groups? Where?
- Purity is a priority, so we'll set these boundaries:

_____

- We'll support one another by listening, cheering, encouraging, and showing loyalty.
- We'll understand it's healthy to hang out with other friends ___ times a week.
- We'll bring out the best in one another through acceptance, faith, and respect.

Once your parents agree and you've covered some key questions, consider these free or inexpensive activities to do together:

- Outings at a local park
- Playing board games
- Walks
- Movie nights
- Youth group
- Community projects, like cleaning a local waterway
- Bike rides
- Window shopping
- Cooking
- Studying

All the best relationships start with friendship. The Bible says a key ingredient to friendship is loyalty. To go deeper with a guy, you've got to be loyal, honest, and trustworthy. The best relationships take time to develop. Be patient, but be active.

WORD OF TRUTH

A friend is always loyal, and a brother is born to help in time of need.
PROVERBS 17:17

Get in the Action

Hollywood action stars are amazing in their movies. With fierce determination, they run into burning buildings, cling to flying airplanes, or jump into freezing rivers to save a girl in distress.

As guys, we want to believe that we'd do the same thing. But statistics show that most guys are passive. They hang back instead of taking action. And it's not just a problem today . . . it started with the very first man.

If you grew up going to Sunday school, you've probably seen pictures of Eve being tempted by the serpent in the Garden of Eden. As the snake slithers down the beautifully fruited tree, Eve looks entranced by Satan's temptations. We all know what happens next: Eve eats the fruit.

But have you ever asked, "Where was Adam?" The Bible has the answer. He was right there with her, and he didn't do a thing! Adam wasn't off naming animals or hunting down dinner. According to Genesis 3:6, Eve took the fruit, ate it, gave it to Adam—who was with her—and he ate it too.

Adam could've taken the fruit from Eve's hand and tossed it away before it touched her lips. Even better, he could've grabbed a stick and stabbed the serpent until its forked tongue lay limp. Instead Adam, "who was with her," stood back and did nothing as sin entered the world.

As guys, we can't follow Adam's example. We need to be men of action. We need to take the lead when it comes to living for Christ, having high standards for the entertainment we watch, and protecting the girls in our lives. God doesn't want us living lame lives. He wants us to live supernaturally—determined to make a difference in the world for him.

We may lack the rippling muscles of an action star, but we can take action and be a star in our own right.

WORD OF TRUTH

She took some of the fruit and ate it. Then she gave some to her husband, who was with her, and he ate it, too.

GENESIS 3:6

Girl talk

Excuses—
Everybody Has One

A guy calls and asks you to the movies Friday night. That's great—except you really don't like him. Instead of being straightforward, you give an excuse. Check any that you've used:

☐ I have to wash my hair.
☐ I promised to babysit our neighbor's iguana.
☐ I have too much homework.
☐ I have to feed my cat.
☐ I have to clean my room.
☐ I'm donating blood that afternoon and will be too dizzy.
☐ It's my little sister's best friend's aunt's birthday.

Excuses can get us out of things we don't want to do. But they also keep us in situations that it'd be best to get out of. Have you ever used an excuse to stay in a relationship when you knew it wasn't working?

☐ I don't want to be alone.
☐ I don't want to hurt his feelings.
☐ He'll change.

Excuses justify our behavior. But they aren't always honest. Often they require us to lie to someone else or to ourselves.

Jesus didn't like excuses. He told a story about a man who invited people to a special dinner. But instead of guests, the man received a bunch of excuses.

- "I need to look at land I just bought."
- "I have to try out my new oxen."
- "I just got married."

The master wanted the party to go on. He quickly sent his servant to invite other people—the poor and handicapped, anyone who would come. His tables were filled. Not with the excuse makers, but with people who accepted the master's invitation (see Luke 14:15-24).

Jesus' story was about people who rejected his call. But he also made a great point about excuses: they can cause us to miss out on something amazing.

Don't hide behind excuses. Be honest with yourself and with the guys in your life. They prefer a straight answer, but one delivered kindly. When you avoid excuses, you'll have no excuse not to pursue healthy relationships.

WORD OF TRUTH

They all began making excuses. One said, "I have just bought a field and must inspect it. Please excuse me."
LUKE 14:18

Guy talk

Not a Fair Fight

If you were to arm wrestle your girl friends or girlfriend, who would win?

You would, right? Most guys have a physical advantage when it comes to arm wrestling a girl. Our arms are longer. Our wrists are broader. Our muscles are stronger. Plus, you'd have a ton of adrenaline from holding hands with a girl. *Ha!*

But if you were to get into a war of words with a girl, who would come out on top? Probably the girl. Most girls have a verbal advantage when it comes to arguing. They speak more proficiently and passionately. They're better at expressing emotion. They have a greater vocabulary.

Because we're no match for a girl when it comes to vocal "wrestling," some guys turn to dirty tactics. We call names. We get angry and start shouting. We shut down and don't say anything. Or we get physical, especially in romantic relationships.

The statistics are startling. According to recent research, one out of three fourteen-year-olds has experienced physical, sexual, or psychological abuse in a dating relationship. That number jumps up to nearly half of people experiencing some kind of violence in a dating relationship before they graduate college.

When we're losing a war of words, it's easy to get angry. As guys, we don't show many emotions, so we often turn to anger pretty quickly. But the Bible tells us not to sin in our anger (see Ephesians 4:26). That means name-calling or getting physical should never be options.

If you feel yourself getting frustrated in a verbal exchange with a girl, simply walk away. Remove yourself from the situation (and from her) before things escalate. Then work to regain your calm. Some guys listen to music, go on a drive, or work out to deal with their feelings. Find what works for you.

As guys, we need to control our tempers. If we constantly explode, girls are going to keep their distance (and they should). So keep cool and fight fair . . . even if that means walking away.

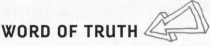

WORD OF TRUTH

Control your temper, for anger labels you a fool.
ECCLESIASTES 7:9

War of Words

for Guys & Girls

You did it again. You ended up in a fight with that special person in your life.

When two sinful humans try to have a relationship, the results aren't always pretty. Arguments will happen, so we have to learn to fight fair . . . and not escalate the situation.

If you're a guy, maybe you shouted, gave an ultimatum, or shut down and stopped talking.

If you're a girl, perhaps you yelled, cried, got dramatic, or stomped off in a huff.

No matter who did what to whom, you might be thinking, *Why can't he/she see things my way?*

And those thoughts may be part of the problem. We all want things our way, whether we admit it or not. Thinking of *me* is easy; thinking of others is hard.

You won't always agree on everything in a relationship. If you did, that could get boring.

Friday
Guy: I was thinking we'd go eat sushi tonight.
Girl: Me too.

Saturday
Guy: Hmmm, sushi sounds good.
Girl: I was thinking the same.

Sunday

Guy: How about some sushi for lunch?
Girl: Sounds great!

See? Boring. Disagreements can bring passion to a relationship. Not all arguments are bad. But fights should never get physically or verbally abusive. If they do, break off the relationship right away and tell a parent or other trusted adult what happened.

To have a healthy relationship, it's good to develop healthy conflict resolution skills. When tempers flare, start by getting a grip on your feelings. Take an honest look at your desires and what role you played in the argument.

Then make space for yourself to calm down. It's hard to settle things until the wave of emotions has become more tranquil.

Finally, be open to finding the best way—not just your way. Plan a time to sit and discuss the problem. It might be in fifteen minutes or the next day. Then follow these steps.

10 Steps to Resolve Conflicts

1. Meet when tempers have relaxed. Getting together in a public place can help keep a discussion under control.
2. Identify and define the problem. Stick to the *one* issue without bringing in other issues or past problems.
3. List each person's desires, needs, and reasons for taking a certain position. Admit any selfish desires. State facts (guys tend to go there) but also express emotional desires (a must for girls).
4. Brainstorm possible solutions.
5. Be flexible and open-minded in listening to ideas. But be firm when it comes to convictions or matters of faith.

6. List pros and cons of each proposed solution and how you'll each benefit.
7. Offer to pray together. Forgive one another for words said in anger during the fight.
8. Choose one solution to try. Agree to give it your best effort.
9. Set a time to evaluate how the solution worked.
10. Meet at the agreed time and evaluate the outcome. If needed, look for a new solution.

Once you settle on an action plan or resolve the issue, relax and let go. Disagreements are part of a relationship, and so is making up. So . . .

- Enjoy a walk or treat.
- Watch a movie you both enjoy.
- Hug.
- Laugh together.

Some people seek conflict. Others avoid it. But everybody should strive to resolve it quickly and in a way that honors God.

WORD OF TRUTH

What is causing the quarrels and fights among you? Don't they come from the evil desires at war within you?
JAMES 4:1

Let Us Pray

Prayer is personal. We share our thoughts, admit our mistakes, ask for our needs to be met, and praise God for his goodness.

Prayer can also be public. We pray together at meals and in youth group to thank God for his blessings.

Prayer is a powerful tool for communicating with God. And here's the cool part: God always hears and answers our prayers. Keeping a prayer journal can show us how God is active in our lives and in the lives of our family and friends.

Prayer is good, but it can be dangerous . . . if guys and girls do it alone. Prayer is intimate. It binds us together with God and with the person we pray with. If we're praying alone with a guy, especially late at night, it can lead to other "less spiritual" activities.

To protect yourself, it's probably best to pray only in group settings with guys. Take turns praying before meals. Prayers can be simple, thanking God for food and health. At youth group or in other gatherings, we can suggest these ideas:

Prayer Circle

Join hands to form a circle. Let one person start with a one-sentence prayer. The person praying squeezes the hand of the next person. That person says a prayer aloud or silently and squeezes the next hand. Continue around the circle until the last prayer is prayed. When the hand of the first person is squeezed, everyone ends with a resounding *amen*.

Prayer Slips

Put out a basket, slips of paper, and pens. Everyone who wants to can write a praise or prayer request and drop the slip into the basket. Those who filled out a slip—or people who want to pray—take one before leaving the meeting and pray for the needs or praises written on the slip.

A popular pastor once said, "No prayer, no power. Little prayer, little power. Much prayer, much power." The Bible encourages us to pray constantly. That's good advice . . . so pray a lot.

WORD OF TRUTH

Whenever I pray, I make my requests for all of you with joy.
PHILIPPIANS 1:4

Guy talk

Don't Hide, Just Decide

We aren't born great decision makers. Just ask your parents about some of the things you decided to do as a child. Maybe you . . .

- ☐ picked a pinecone (or something worse) off the ground and jammed it into your mouth.
- ☐ ran around outside naked.
- ☐ dove headfirst down the stairs.
- ☐ bit people when you got mad.
- ☐ stuck your fingers into the electrical outlet.

None of those is a good decision or a socially acceptable behavior. Decision making is like weight lifting. The more reps we do, the stronger we become. In weight lifting, a good spotter makes sure we don't get crushed by the weight. Just like in weight lifting, we need to choose our decision-making spotter wisely. Bouncing things off a good friend and always including God are good ideas.

Some guys hide from decisions. They figure if they avoid making a decision, then they can't make a wrong one. But that just keeps us stuck . . . and weak.

Girls have a hard time respecting weak guys. They want a strong decision maker. Work on your decision-making abilities by following this workout plan:

1. Gather information by researching the pros and cons of a decision. Ask for advice from older siblings, parents, and friends.

2. Figure out what's most important to you. Sometimes professional athletes don't sign with the team that offers the most money. If they like a city, a coach, or certain teammates, it could make the difference. Make a list of your deal breakers and deal makers.
3. Pray. Ask God for wisdom. The Bible tells us God doesn't get mad when we ask for wisdom. He wants us to tap into his power.
4. Make the best choice for you. And once you decide, move forward with your plan.

The weight of some decisions will test us more than others. When the hard decisions come, make sure to be thoughtful, prayerful, and careful.

WORD OF TRUTH

If you need wisdom, ask our generous God, and he will give it to you. He will not rebuke you for asking.
JAMES 1:5

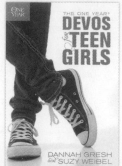

DIVE DEEPER
into God's Word with these
DEVOTIONALS FOR TEENS!

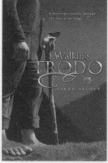